T-CELLS & SYMPATHY

T-CELLS & SYMPATHY
Monologues in the Age of AIDS

Michael Kearns

HEINEMANN
Portsmouth, NH

Heinemann
A division of Reed Elsevier Inc.
361 Hanover Street
Portsmouth, NH 03801-3912

Offices and agents throughout the world

Library of Congress Cataloging-in-Publication Data

Kearns, Michael, 1950–
    T-cells & sympathy : monologues in the age of AIDS / Michael Kearns.
      p. cm.
    ISBN 0-435-08676-6
    1. AIDS (Disease)–Patients–United States–Drama.
2. Monologues. I. Title II. Title: T-cells and sympathy
PS3561.E246T2 1995
812'.54–dc20   95-17109
                                                        CIP

Performance rights information can be found at the end of this book.

Editor: Lisa A. Barnett
Production: Vicki Kasabian
Text design: Tom Allen, Pear Graphic Design
Cover design: Gwen Frankfeldt
Cover photograph: Jon Nickson/The Fringe
Author photograph: Richard Bomersheim

Printed in the United States of America on acid-free paper
99 98 97 96 95 DA 1 2 3 4 5

Contents

ROBERT'S MEMORIAL

DISCO DAZE

Introduction

U NLESS A CURE FOR AIDS IS IMMEDIATE, allowing me to continue writing into my sixties and seventies, I realistically regard *T-Cells & Sympathy* as the bulk of my life's work. More than the television guest spots, the talk show appearances, the hundreds of articles, this collection of thirty-four monologues is me. If asked, "What did you do in the war, Daddy?" I'll answer, "I wrote AIDS monologues." Breathing life into a disease which might kill me wasn't an option; my heart and soul and guts dictated I must. AIDS was the catalyst that led me to find my voice as an actor and a writer; the monologue became the vessel.

By the time I began studying the Stanislavski Method at Marian Epstein's Junior Theatre in St. Louis, prior to my tenth birthday, I had perfected the art of lip-synching to two theatrical masterpieces: Professor Harold Hill's recitative on the evils of playing pool ("Trouble" from *The Music Man*) and Mama Rose's show biz aria on the evils of stage motherhood ("Rose's Turn" from *Gypsy*). While other boys my age were swinging bats and chasing girls, I was holed up in my basement with a record player (that's what we called them in those days) and Broadway soundtracks, mouthing and gesticulating myself into an adrenalin-pumped frenzy. "Some people got it and make it pay," I (as Rose) would effuse, "and some people can't even give it away."

What attracted me to these particular pieces was the intensity of the words and the larger-than-lifeness of the characters, which resulted in an overpowering connection with the audience. In my case, an underground (literally), imaginary audience. These weren't really show-stopping songs as much as they were gutsy monologues. Little did I realize, as I wore out those records from relentless rehearsing, the monologue would become my primary form of expression as an actor and a writer.

I didn't reveal my lip-synching skills to Miss Epstein who, in her sleek blue-gray suits with hair to match, was much too weighty for musical comedy. Controversial in her approach, she determinedly taught aspiring child thespians how to feel their emotions from the inside out. "You much *become* the character," she'd preach in the baritone voice of a seasoned grande dame.

What Miss Epstein also taught her impressionable wards was something I could neither pronounce nor spell at the time: empathy. "Never look for what's different than you in another human being; look for how you are similar," she'd alternately bark or coo, depending on her fluctuating moods. In order to act, she'd further insist, you must "use your true self."

During the ensuing twenty years, I lip-synched less and monologued more—from Shakespeare to Miller, from Ibsen to Williams—always attempting to follow Miss Epstein's golden rules. The monologue, however, because it was always associated with the act of auditioning ("Prepare two monologues, one classical and one contemporary") became an enemy to be feared, not loved.

It wasn't until I saw Harry Hart-Browne's *Pardon Me, I'm Having an Emotion,* that I renewed my love affair with the form. Not only was Harry's extended monologue brimming with jaunty humor, it was surprisingly gay. Keep in mind, gay one-person shows were scarce in the late seventies; Hart-Browne was a pioneer.

My next association with a one-man show was Rob Sullivan's *Flower Ladies and Pistol Kids,* a decidedly heterosexual and luminously autobiographical piece, which I produced in 1980. The following year, I appeared in the West Coast premiere of Harvey Fierstein's *The International Stud* (part one of *Torch Song Trilogy*), which gave me the opportunity to immerse myself in one of the most searing theatrical monologues ever written; Arnold, the ultimate drama drag queen, perched in front of a mirror, addresses the audience as he readies him/herself for an extravagant entrance. This was more fun that Professor Harold Hill and Mama Rose combined; it was also the most committed—albeit, not completely drug- and alcohol-free—work of my career.

In 1982, I entered a recovery program for chemical dependency: an act that saved my life as well as my art. During the first tumultuous year of my newfound sobriety, I felt compelled to write a theatrical monologue as an act of self-preservation. This was after having established myself as a qualified journalist, primarily of entertainment profiles. That solo work, *The Truth Is Bad Enough,* in which I attempted to understand the profligacy of the seventies, including my surreal stint as the "author" of a hoax called *The Happy Hustler,* premiered in 1983. A modest success, in spite of the cathartic self-indulgence, no one denied my first "written and performed by" piece was a testament to unbridled theatricality.

From then on, like everyone in Hollywood, I became typed: the openly gay actor who does one-man shows. Playwright James Carroll Pickett, aftering seeing *Truth,* approached me with his bravura *Bathhouse Benediction.* While I was a tad young to act the role of a fortyish, doomed hero, I jumped at the chance to direct my first monologue instead.

The following year (1985), I was given a gift that would change the course of my career: the title role of the histrionic hustler in Pickett's *Dream Man,* a character I would intermittently play all over the world for the next several years. In retrospect, I'm convinced it was the religious-like experience of repeatedly performing Pickett's gorgeous language that liberated and ignited my untapped writer self.

While *Dream Man* did not directly tackle AIDS, it was written as AIDS emerged and loomed disturbingly prophetic. In addition to *Dream Man,* I became associated with the rash of AIDS plays that were beginning to emerge, including the sexually charged political eruptions of Robert Chesley. As a director, diving into the ribald, uninhibited brilliance of Chesley's *Jerker* granted me permission to avoid squeamishness about any aspect of human sexuality when I would begin writing. Within a few months, I was classified as a gay actor/director who did AIDS plays.

When Rock Hudson died in late 1985, I publicly castigated Hollywood for its reprehensible homophobia and experienced a dramatic decrease in my income from the television and film industry that had heretofore supported my theatre habit. Now I was forced to make a living as an openly gay artist doing so-called AIDS theatre.

As my friends began dying, I forged a life on the road, performing (in addition to *Dream Man*) monologues written by other contemporary gay writers: Chesley, Doug Holsclaw, Rebecca Ranson. I would always include an excerpt from *The Truth Is Bad Enough,* the only self-written theatrical piece in my repertoire at that time.

As the names of the deceased increased, my passion and my politics merged. While they were of enormous importance and comfort, I began to weary of the so-called AIDS plays that continued to focus solely on the issues of the gay, white male—even though the activists among us were in the streets screaming that AIDS was not confined to the gay, white community.

I decided to write a performance piece for myself, concentrating on people with AIDS who were not being represented in the theatre, or in the media, period. While it had been more than five years since I wrote *The Truth Is Bad Enough,* this writing experience was head-to-toes organic; all the elements were poised to coalesce. The ingested words of my muses—from Miss Epstein's lectures on empathy to Pickett's sinewy poetry—guided me.

Tim Miller provided the glue; not only did he always encourage me to join the ranks of performance artists, he provided me with a theatre. In the spring of 1989, *intimacies* opened at Highways Performance Space in Los Angeles, an experience so powerful, it would define the next five years of my artistic life. The monologues proved to be the perfect vehicle for the marriage of my writing and acting abilities, empowering my activist approach. Not only did I cast myself in roles no one else would dare (a female, African American hooker, for example), but I was able to create landscapes that I felt were necessary to humanize AIDS beyond the gay white male ghetto. I love the monologue's immediacy and, yes, intimacy. The form doesn't allow an audience to sit back; it invites—no, *demands*—participation. In *intimacies* and *more intimacies,* I force the viewer to consider the fact that those with HIV/AIDS—in spite of race, age, sexual orientation, gender, or class—are still people; they are not a disease. Most of the gallery of characters do not address their illness; in ten minutes or so, I challenge myself, as an actor-writer, to capture the depth and breadth of a three-act play.

How do the characters evolve? Each is birthed individually, including a gestation period—from the moment I conceive the character to the moment I begin writing it. During that intense period, ranging anywhere from a few days to a few months, I become the character (as an actor), inhabiting the rhythm, the voice, the stance as well as the story.

While my stable of characters has been performed by actors other than gay white men, the metaphor of a GWM "becoming" (read: empathizing with) those who are *different than* is absolutely intentional. The questionable political correctness of a white actor playing an African American or a hearing actor playing a deaf character or a man playing a woman is not only deliberately controversial, it has become my modus operandi. As an adolescent, there was no question I possessed the damaged goods to infuse Mama Rose; Miss Epstein reinforced the actor's ability—no, responsibility—to play all things human.

All writing is inevitably from one's experience, no matter how strongly imagination dominates the writer's palette.

While autobiography colors every piece I've ever written, the hues spring from invention. This is where my mother deserves credit. In my recollection, never did my mother simply see things as they were; she provided generous plot to the most pedantic tableaux. Observing a woman waiting for a bus, my mother would—based on how the woman was dressed or how she held herself—wax eloquent about her life. "She's going somewhere to be noticed," she'd say, or "She's just been involved in a fight and she's on the run." While I never studied writing formally, my mother imbued me with a keen hunger to connect the dots of human behavior.

So *Rock* (1992) was less of a departure than it appeared, although I overtly mixed fact and fiction, legend and myth, biography and autobiography, including the announcement of my HIV-positive status on national television. More performance-arty in concept and execution, some insiders noted that *Rock* was a subtle sequel to *The Truth Is Bad Enough*.

As I continued to perform these pieces all over the world, I began writing a three-character play. While not without its share of monologues, *Myron* was my first dance with dialogue. Although I initially conceived and wrote *off* and *Robert's Memorial* as solo pieces, my desire to perform was being eclipsed by my overriding need to write. It became time to feed the material to other actors.

For the first time in my life, I described myself as a "writer who acts," not an "actor who writes." This redefining of myself holds greater implications than simply making a career move. It has allowed me to fulfill one of my life's long overdue desires: parenting. As I spent more time in front of the computer and less time on the stage, I made room to become a licensed foster parent and welcomed a number of children into my heart and home. The sounds of life, after more than a decade of death's melodies, have rejuvenated me.

What will evolve artistically, based on my personal momentum, remains liberatingly open. While writing is what nourishes me most completely, I feel it's time to venture beyond the monologue, even though it will remain my most cherished form of expression.

I have been called many things in my career—from monologuist to performance artist—but "solo performer" label seems the most misleading since I have not accomplished anything alone. In addition to all of the abovementioned, there is a triumvirate of creative souls who have lovingly lavished me with personal and professional support: Kelly Hill, who acted as dramaturge as well as director on *intimacies, more intimacies,* and *Rock;* Darien Martus, who creates original music for almost all of my work; Raymond Thompson, who lights me whenever I can get him. They have been my artistic family.

While I'm in the Oscar acceptance speech mode, I must also acknowledge the presenters who have provided homes away from home and put bread and butter on my table: Tim and everyone at Highways; Pat Sheehy at the Source Theatre in D.C.; Sarah Shelley, formerly of Humboldt State; Portland's Howie Bagadonutz, Will K. Wilkins of Real Art Ways, Donald Montwill at Josie's in S.F.; Joan Lipkin in my hometown of St. Louis; Karen Skinner at the Circle Theatre in Forest Park, Illinois; Gillian Minervini in Sydney, Australia.

In conclusion, I feel blessed to have made music with the monologue: an outlet for the indignities and enlightenments, the illuminations and ruminations, the hysteria and the serenity I've experienced living and loving and laughing during a plague.

Michael Kearns
Los Angeles, 1995

THE TRUTH IS BAD ENOUGH

Michael

Michael is a thirtysomething gay male.

(Directly addressing audience) I meet Victor. An actor. A Cuban actor. Lucy fell in love with a Cuban actor. Look what happened to her. *(To an imaginary Victor)* Victor, I'm in love with you. This is it; nothing else compares. When we make love, it's like the first time. I've never wanted to be inside someone; I've never wanted someone inside me. Until now. I never knew I could love like this. Of course, I never thought I could stay sober for year, either. Victor, what can I say? I wanna marry you! What does my sponsor think? I haven't even told him yet. *(To an imaginary Al)* Al, I know it's not a good idea to replace drugs and alcohol with a man. Especially an actor. Especially a Cuban actor. Especially a Cuban actor who already has a lover. But he's going to split up with him. He promises. It takes time. You're the one who taught me to be patient. Understanding. Serene. *(To Victor)* Victor, for Chrissakes, it's been four fucking months. I can't wait another fucking minute. I'm sick of playing Susan Hayward to your Ricky Ricardo. You've got to make a decision. You know what, Victor? I could learn to hate you. *(To Al)* Remember when Victor left the lover and decided he didn't want me either? I thought I'd die. Or drink. Or shoot up. It was the first time in my life I cried—really cried—as an adult. While I was crying, I decided to hate him. I chose to hate. I'm going to be sober two years tomorrow and I still hate people. I still hate my father. I still hate Victor. I guess what I'm trying to say is: Help! *(To Victor, on phone)* Victor? Hello. It's Michael. Yeah, it's been a long time. Almost two years. I see you on TV. One night I was watching television with this guy, mak-

ing out on his couch. He was the first person I considered getting serious with since you. And guess who shows up on *Dynasty?* You were adorable, but the entire night I kept seeing your face, your arms, your chest. He smelled like you, tasted like you. When he talked dirty, it was with a Cuban accent. I just want you to know I don't hate you. I'm not sure I ever loved you, either, but I don't hate you. I don't know what love is. *(To audience)* If I could let go of my hatred for Victor, I knew it was time to say goodbye to my father. I visited him in St. Louis. *(To Al)* Al, he's an old man. Eighty years old. Bedridden. But alert. He knew me. Heard every word. Between seeing my father and seeing so many friends dying of AIDS, I am so in touch with my mortality. At least I'm sober. Three years tomorrow. Thank God I didn't die drunk. You know what? I love you. You're more of a father than my real father. *(To Victor, on phone)* Victor, honey. I heard. When were you diagnosed? Do you want me to come see you? I know I don't have to; I want to. *(To Al)* We went Christmas shopping at the Beverly Center. He's blind in one eye and he's lost a lot of weight but he's in pretty good shape otherwise. It was awkward at first but we remember being comfortable together. *(To Victor)* Remember my sponsor, Al? He had a stroke. He's in the hospital, undergoing physical therapy. Speaking of physical therapy, how about a foot massage? *(To Al)* I thought you'd be out of here by now. Victor? He's getting worse. He's totally blind. Bedridden. I'm going to spend one night a week with him. I used to wonder whether or not I loved him. Now I know. Al, thank God you don't have AIDS. *(To Victor)* My sponsor was diagnosed: P. M. L. The one that plays havoc with your brain. He's losing his mind— literally. I'm happy to be here with you, too, sweetheart. I've missed my baby. *(To Al)* Here, Al, take a bite of strawberry. You love strawberries, don't you? *(To Victor)* Shall we change your diaper, sweetheart? *(To Al)* The nurse thought I was your son. She assures me you can hear me, Al, even though you can't respond. Don't even try to say anything. I guess it's time for me to say goodbye. I'm going to miss you. I'm going to miss all those fish 'n chip lunches in Silverlake. I'm going to miss being the baby. You've helped me turn my life around. You've watched me grow up. If I can face this, I can face just about anything. *(To Victor)* Are you asleep, honey? You're tired, aren't you? And humiliated. Don't be. Please. All I ever wanted from you was intimacy and intensity. These past few weeks have taken intimacy and intensity to heights I could never have imagined. To be able to love you while you're growling like a wounded puppy and losing control like a newborn baby has been a gift. You've taught me how to love. That's something I thought I was incapable of. Al died last week. I know you're going to go soon. Probably tomorrow. But I'll be with you again. Somewhere. I'm not going to say goodbye. I know you're looking forward to it—whatever "it" is. So good luck. Wish me luck, too.

intimacies

Denny

Denny is fortyish, suffering from dementia.

Don't talk to me about gay brotherhood, girlfriend. They wish I was dead. I'm the type that gives gay liberation a bad name. My name, by the way, is Denny, but you can call me Creme Dementia. These fuckin' hospital slippers won't click, click, click. There's no place like homeless; there's no place like homeless; there's no place like homeless. Benefits for homeless and AIDS and alkies—oh, my! I'm a walking telethon, girlfriend. But I ain't seen a leftover quiche from any of Cleopatra's parties. So I'm producin' my own. (*Sings*) "Please don't talk about love tonight . . ." This is my farewell tour, honey. (*Sings*) "Please don't talk about sweeeet love . . ." Don't tell George Bush: I use American flags for diapers. Then I burn 'em. If you think I'm demented now, honey, you should have seen me then. I was sooo demented . . . I was sooo demented, I shot up crystal and went to brunch with the family on Mother's Day. (*Sings*) "I'll always love my Mama 'cause she's my favorite girl . . ." I don't have twenty-five cents for the fuckin' pay phone and these fuckin' fags have phones in their Jeeps. I asked one of 'em to call my agent. My travel agent. Book me a spiritual plane. To the big death valley. Spare me the faith healers and prayer meetings. The idea of a new miracle drug is about as exciting to me as . . . Calvin Klein underwear. I'm ready for my closeup, Mr. Undertaker. If my T-cells get any lower, I'm gonna name the motherfuckers. They tell me I'm suffering from OBS— Obnoxiously Bad Sex. Calvin Klein underwear. I was sooo demented . . . I was sooo demented, I wore a butt plug to my tenth year high school reunion. I've been writing my will. I have only three requests: bury me with my tambourine; no Stephen Sondheim songs; send all donations to Save The Baths. I love this new expression: Self Delivery. I went to the Post Office and asked how much. "How much would you charge to self deliver me?" You shoulda seen the bitch's face. "I'll have to ask my supervisor." Now this big black stud is standin' there—more chains around his neck than Sammy Davis, Jr. on an opening night. "You want to what?" "I want to suck on your big black hard piece of meat, honey." Then I ran out onto the street. And this big buck is chasin' me. I start screamin' "Rape! Rape!" at the top of my damaged lungs. Well, it worked. Of course people believed this mean black dude was chasin' this glamorous white woman. So he stopped, realizin' he'd be tarred and feathered before I would. Besides, he probably figured I'd like to be tarred and feathered. And he's right! As long as the feathers match this hospital gown. I'm thinking about getting into the phone sex business: 976-DEAD. Maybe I'll answer, maybe I won't. You all heard of the Names Project. That's me, tryin' to remember my old boyfriends. Calvin Klein underwear. In case you're wonderin', I'm open to another marriage but the only man who'd marry me is hooked up to an oxygen machine and can't possibly say "I do." I don't regret one of my marriages and I lost track somewhere in the 1970s. There isn't one inch of my slightly deteriorated body that hasn't been pinched or punched or poked or prodded. How many of you can say that? When they came in me, they stayed in me. They left souvenirs: damaged childhoods, fucked up adolescences, disapproving parents and outraged wives. I don't believe their bodily fluids gave me AIDS. We been poisoned by something but not bodily fluids. We been poisoned by hate, hate from Moms and Dads and uncles and aunts and priests and nuns and school systems and mayors and the Moral Fucking Majority and Miss Jesse Helms and Calvin Klein underwear and the Reagan Fucking Administrations. Bodily fluids gave me life, honey. Hatred is what's killin' me. Oh, yeah, I read those lists: No, Don't, Stop. I would have died without bodily fluids. I refused to abstain. The only thing harder to put on than false eyelashes is a fuckin' rubber. I needed to feel their semen settlin' in my soul, their spit activatin' my heart. Making me alive. I even indulged in an occasional piss cocktail now and then. That's a sure cure for any of yous sufferin' from fear of intimacy. You probably won't read about me in *People* magazine or see me on *Nightline*. Besides, I don't have a thing to wear. I traded in my La Coste shirts for a hospital gown. Tried to get into Studio One the other night but they didn't like my hospital slippers. Get real, girleen. So I stood outside. Some big burley number with a sissy voice told me to split. "Listen here, you overripe piece of fruit, I'm a safe sex advertisement; havin' to look at me is better than any of those keep-your-tongue-outta-buttholes lists. You'll have to carry me away, Mr. Big Stuff." (*Sings*) "Mr. Big Stuff, who do you think you are?" Listen, honeys, windin' up like this was not my life's ambition. When I was a young and pretty—younger and prettier—I went to the parties with the gay elite, the gay effete. I took the same drugs and sat on the same cocks. Some are just luckier than others. (*Sings*) "I love the nightlife, I love to boogie . . ."

Big Red

Big Red is a female black street hooker, late thirties.

Between hand jobs, I concentrate on forgiveness. That's all I
got time for these days. It's jus' a matter of time. I been lucky.
I got a few lesions on my head and this tiny one on my face.
I'm special! Most womens don't get lesions: that's what they
tole me at the clinic. Little bitch who tole me was makin' a
point, knowin' my profession. Lesions is God's way of punishin' a whore like me, she was sayin'. I don't believe that shit.
How'd I get it? How long have I had it? Now what the fuck
difference does it make? Probably from a drug addict. Or
maybe up the ole poop shoot. You'd be surprised how many
guys hire a whore so they can act like they're a faggot. "Suck
my dick; let me fuck you in the ass." I made my tricks wear
rubbers back when AIDS was somethin' I took to keep the
weight off. But, sure, there were times when the fuckin'
things broke. You hear me? Uh, huh. And there mighta been
a few druggies shootin' up—you never know about that.
And, yeah, I forgot. I forget a lot these days. It might be the
disease. Uh, huh. Walter. Now he swears he ain't got it but he
ain't been tested neither. We got back together a few years
ago. He's the only man I ever loved so I'd like to think I got it
from love and not from some druggie stranger who popped
open a rubber. You hear me? Uh, huh. Walter could be the
one. He's been shootin' drugs mosta his life. And fuckin' with
transsexuals. And transvestites. I don't know which is which.
Sometimes I think that's why he comes back to me: I can
suck dick and I dress like a drag queen. Uh, huh. First time I
got paid to suck dick I was eleven or twelve years old. This
nasty uncle—my mother's brother—paid me to keep my

mouth shut. I mean, to keep my mouth wide open, then shut up tight. I was a quick learner. Probably because I liked it. I liked the feel of warmth shootin' inside me. And I liked the cash. I liked bein' good at somethin'. Eventually, I started givin' blow jobs to teenage punks in a downtown movie theatre. I'd be lucky to get a box of jujubes. But I liked it. That's where I met Walter. I was fourteen. He was a few years older. A real tough guy. Juvenile delinquent. He liked to watch me go down on his buddies as much as he liked gettin' it hisself. Some guys—now, baby, this might surprise you—some guys, they need a finger up their butt to keep it hard. Walter was one of them guys. He even liked a finger up there when he fucked me. Which he did—not at the movie theatre, in his car, where one of his nasty friends would watch. I married him. Four or five months pregnant at the time. Got a ten-year-old daughter to prove it. Farrah. My one and only baby child. Walter went to jail when she was a baby and my mama had to raise her. I hit the streets and I been here ever since. Uh, huh. You must wonder why I can't get off these streets. Listen, I ain't doin' nothin' dangerous. You hear me? Jus' hand jobs these days. Most I can make is twenty, thirty bucks. How many hand jobs will it take to send Farrah to college? Tell ya this: beats the fuck outta bein' a waitress. I tried that—jus' another form of hustlin'. I was lyin' to ya when I tole you I only got one daughter. I got a baby, Annie is her name, and she's only eight months old. One of them popped-open rubbers. Or Walter. Walter could be her Daddy. Jus' couldn't handle it. I can take care of myself, thankyouverymuch, but Annie's in bad shape. She and I got somethin' in common. You know. Wears a colostomy bag, that tiny baby. Weighs less than a pair of my high heels. That disease is in her. It's jus' a matter of time. Oh, she's okay right now. Livin' in a big, beautiful house with a big, strong lady who wouldn't have no babies of her own. Right after Annie was born, I started gettin' chemotherapy. My hair started fallin' out by the handful. I bet you already figured this is not my real hair. A bald whore is worse than a diseased whore. You don't always see the disease. God has been good to me. Gave me a beautiful head of red hair. My best feature. Some guys would pay me jus' to tickle their balls with my long, red hair. My hair has been my callin' card. That's my nickname: Big Red, named after my hair. God took that hair back and gave me some beauty marks on my head. That's what I call 'em: beauty marks. And one tiny beauty mark on my face. God knew I could buy a wig. God knows I need to keep workin' so I can send money to Farrah's grandma who takes care of her. They don't know I'm sick. Farrah don't know she's got a dyin' baby sister. Secrets. I keep secrets. My mother, Farrah's grandma, she knew her brother was payin' me to have sex. I keep so many secrets. If I was gonna start blamin' people for my life, I guess I'd start there. But what's the point? Huh? Big Red is gonna keep on truckin'. God ain't punishin' me. How could he punish a baby like Annie and not punish my mama for encouragin' her own daughter to become a slut? That don't make much sense now, does it? I jus' try to forgive my Mama. She promises me she's not pervertin' Farrah and I gotta believe her. And forgive that nasty uncle. And Walter. Or the asshole who broke open the rubber. Whoever gave me these beauty marks and a baby born to die. It's jus' a matter of time. You hear me? Time for forgiveness. Who knows? Maybe someday I'll forgive . . . Forget that. I ain't got that much time left.

Patrick

Patrick is a gay beauty clone, thirtyish.

Shortly after I had my chin implant, I told this guy my name was Patrick and he said, "Did you say 'Perfect?'" I'm close to perfect. I paid for it; I wasn't born this way. Teeth, nose, cheekbones: all done. Best haircutter in the city. And I go to the gym—three hours a day, seven days a week. Easy to imagine someone thought my name is Perfect. Being perfect ain't easy. I work at it. I also have the perfect car, condo, and closet full of clothes. Barry, my lover, is also perfect: rich, gorgeous, powerful. We're in the entertainment industry. He's an agent at William Morris; I'm an accountant at Disney. Perfect. People are always saying I look like I'm an actor but that's just because I'm gay. Not that I'm completely out of the closet. Neither is Barry. I mean, we're out. Except to our parents. And at work. We even take dates to office functions. We have to; it's just part of the Hollywood game. We don't need to march in gay pride parades or any of that bullshit. We make a yearly donation—$50 each—to AIDS Project. Anonymously. Our lifestyle is really our own business. When I asked about these (*indicating swollen glands*), I really resented my plastic surgeon suggesting I have the test. Look at me; do I look sick? Barry and I have been together for seven years. "Has it been a monogamous relationship?" the doctor wanted to know. "It's been perfect," I told him. It's really none of the doctor's fucking business. I know Barry has been faithful to me and I've only cheated a coupla times. Not really cheating. Fooling around. The gym. "Do you and your partner have safe sex?" the doctor had the nerve to ask. Of course not. Why would we? We've been together seven years. We're perfectly monogamous—Barry thinks. I can't destroy that. Besides, he might leave me and I can't stand to be alone, for Christ sakes. Barry doesn't like to fuck. I do the fucking in the family so when this really hot guy came on to me at the gym, I let him fuck me. You don't usually carry a condom into the steam room at the Sports Connection, now, do you? It happened at least once a week for several months. It was perfect. He is an actor. To die for. Clean cut. Look at me. Do I look sick? "Fuck it," I said, "I'll take the test." There's no way. No way. Get AIDS in the steam room at the gym, looking the way I do? It's so clean in there. No way. Get serious. When my doctor told me I was positive, I thought he must be kidding. Not me. Look at me. Do I look sick? Then I thought about the actor. He didn't look sick. He couldn't have given it to me; he's a TV star! There was this kid a couple of years ago—maybe it was him. I let him fuck me in the john on the lot at Disney. That was before we knew anything about AIDS. He worked in the mail room. Dick of death. He was black. Even though he was clean, Barry would die. Who? Who gave it to me? I can't be positive. "Are you sure about your lover?" the doctor asked, like he's in some third-rate Movie of the Week. "No," I lied, "it probably is his fault." But I know Barry. He's not a good liar like I am. I'd know. The doctor lectured me about protecting Barry. Immediately. But I can't. I can't tell anyone. And I sure as hell can't tell Barry. Tell him I've given him AIDS for Christmas? C'mon, get serious. The only answer is to kill myself. I never wanted to get old anyway. What's that line? "Live fast, die young, and have a beautiful corpse." I'm just gonna disappear. There'll be no revelations. No screaming parents. No raging lover. No obituary in *Variety* or the *Hollywood Reporter.* No crows'-feet. No fortieth birthday party. No twentieth high school reunion. No tenth year anniversary with Barry. No more lies. No more bullshit. No more plastic surgery. No more hating myself. No more hangovers. No more sex in bushes and johns. No more poppers. No more cocaine. No more steroids. No more. No more. No more. No more hope. Like Norman Maine in *A Star Is Born*, I'm just gonna walk into the Pacific Ocean. At sunset. Judy will be singing in the kitchen. A perfect Hollywood ending. Perfect.

Rusty

Rusty is a teenage street hustler on drugs.

My name is Rusty. Somebody once tole me only hookers, strippers, and lesbians are named Rusty. I am not a lesbian. I'm not really a stripper—not 'til tonight. I got this gig by accident. This fuckin' movie producer picked me up off the street. Fancy fuckin' car. Figured I'd have a place to spend the night. I'd do almost anything for a warm fuckin' bed and twenty bucks. Since Richard left, I been sleepin' in fuckin' cars, in the fuckin' park, under the fuckin' freeway—you name it. Turns out this prissy producer just wants me to dance to some fuckin' disco music from the seventies. I was born in 1970, for Christ sakes. Donna Summer does not get me off. Anyway, I dance. Like I actually like all that love-to-love-you-baby shit. He jerks hisself off—from clear across the room—without even touchin' me. He thought it was so cool I didn't take my shirt off. "That's hot," he kept repeatin'. "That's so hot. Leave your shirt on. Hot. Show me your butt. Show me your dick. Show me your tits. But leave your shirt on. Hot." I guess he thought he was directin' some fuckin' movie. He shot his load all over his fuckin' fat belly and then asked me if I'd be interested in makin' a hundred bucks. That's five times what I'm used to. All I had to do was strip at this party for a bunch of his phoney faggot friends. So here I am. "Keep your shirt on. It's hot," he orders me in that whiny, bitch voice of his. Reminds me of my mother, that voice. "Of course I'll keep my shirt on, you fuckin' asshole. Your fuckin' alcoholic, martini-mouthed priss heads wouldn't want to see track marks on my arms, now, would they?" A hundred bucks would buy me a day's supply a crystal. I usually have to turn five or six tricks a day to survive, keep high. And let me tell you—most of 'em want more than a fuckin' dance routine to some seventies disco beat. One fuckin' maniac actually tried to stick a loaded gun up my butt. Said he wanted to see if I trusted him. Another dude—you mighta read about him in the papers: Doctor Max. He liked to take Polaroid pictures of body parts. Legs, thighs, shoulders, necks. Sounds like I'm orderin' fried chicken, huh? I even let him take a picture of my arms. Track marks and all. Five bucks a shot. He wasn't as squeamish as these Hollywood fags. A few nights later, Doctor Max took a chain saw to Leroy, one of my buddies. Sawed him up and buried the pieces up and down the California coast. I just barely escaped that looney tune. Couldn't dance very well without my legs, now, could I? Only other time I made a hundred bucks was paintin' a house one weekend. I actually tried to get my shit together. Went to this rehab program for street kids. Stopped doin' crystal for about ten days. Had a place to stay. Got this job paintin' houses with this really cool dyke in A.A. I even went to a fuckin' counselor who asked me a million fuckin' questions about my family. You see, my scum-of-the-earth parents kicked me outta the house when they found out I was smokin' dope. They are these fuckin' heavy-duty winos but they go to church every Sunday—after beatin' each other up every Saturday night—so it's okay. If they knew I was fuckin' with guys, they'd shit. If they knew I had the Big A, they'd have a fuckin' heart attack. Which is the one—and only— reason I might tell 'em. What if these holier-than-thou fags found out I got it? One thing is for sure. No fuckin' refunds! That hundred bucks will be dancin' in my veins before the night is over. I've only been on the streets for about a year. Got tested when I was in that rehab place. That did it. Figured I might as well get back on the streets and party. Nobody—nobody—could stop me. Yeah, they taught us all about safe sex. I dare anyone who's shot up crystal to put on a fuckin' rubber. It ain't my responsibility. One of them assholes gave it to me. Right? They ain't all assholes. There is a few cool ones. This one dude, he drives a white Toyota. He took me to see *Rain Man* with that fox Tom Cruise. Now lookin' at him makes me think I'm gay. I fuck girls, too. I'm not sure what I am. The guy who took me to the movies—his name is Richard—all he wanted to do was kiss my eyelids. Jesus. Pretty weird, huh? He bought me this yellow-and-black-checkered shirt—long sleeve—at the Army/Navy Surplus. He taught me to eat with chopsticks. He kissed me on the eyelids—that's all, I swear. He died about four weeks ago. That's when I started gettin' sick. Sometimes the speed makes me sick but this is different. This is it. Richard killed hisself when he found out he got it. I don't got the guts. Whenever I see a white Toyota, I think it's him, gonna save me. His neighbor tole me. I went over there one night—he used to let me sleep on his couch—and his neighbor tole me that Richard hung hisself 'cause he caught AIDS. He handcuffed hisself so he couldn't chicken out and change his mind at the last minute. I went there to have my eyelids kissed. No charge. No shit. Those mother fucking handcuffs. I need to get high. How much longer do I have? To do this fuckin' striptease? What the fuck time is it?

Mary

Mary is a Southern religious fanatic in her sixties.

Holy Mary, mother of God, pray for us sinners now and at the hour of our death. Amen. The hour of our death. Amen. Death. Amen. No matter how far apart, you beat in my heart. Pray for us sinners now and at the hour of our death. You beat in my heart. Amen. It was my turn to receive the valentine this year. We began sending it back and forth in 1974—imagine!—fifteen years ago. David sent it to me in January of '74, the occasion of my first heart attack. It started out as a get well card; it wasn't really designed as a valentine—or a get well card, for that matter. No matter how far apart, you beat in my heart. Seemed like the perfect valentine. So I just found an envelope and returned the card to him on Valentine's Day that year. Then, a year later, on February 14, 1975, he airmailed it back to me. We've cherished it as a yearly valentine ever since—except for the Big One—my 1984 heart attack (five years ago, that's when I was transfused) when it resurfaced as a get well card. No matter how far apart, you beat in my heart. There is ample proof to indicate I will not be alive next Valentine's Day. David does not know this but I must, I must, tell him. And I must return that dilapidated card for the last time. No matter how far apart, you beat in my heart. AIDS is God's punishment. Pray for us sinners now and at the hour of our death. Amen. My sin was in loving my son too much. David was six or seven when I divorced his father. An ugly traumatic parting. His father never paid any attention to him and then tried to prove I was an unfit mother. Unfit? If anything, I overloaded him with love. Whatever Davey wanted, I gave him.

Whatever I could. After his father left, leaving us with next-to-nothing, David became my friend. My best friend. He understood when I had a little too much to drink. He understood my need to find a replacement for his father. Such a good boy. By the time he was nine or ten, he'd stay by himself without a baby-sitter. He'd iron my clothes; I taught him how to hem my skirts. Some Saturday nights, he'd do up my hair. Of course, there were accusations from family members: "Mary, you're turning him into a mama's boy." I didn't pay much attention. I wanted to find a man to help me raise David. Of course, I wanted to find someone to love but nobody loved me as much as that child. Nobody. By the time I did find an excuse for a second husband, David had followed in my footsteps: drinking too much and looking for men. I tried to accept his being homosexual but I knew in my heart it was wrong. I knew it was a sin. A mortal, unforgivable sin. I couldn't accept it—any more than I could accept him marrying a woman. My Davey. Nothing could destroy our bond. God knows I don't love my second husband the way I love David. And I can't accept the idea of his so-called male lovers. The word makes me queasy. Lover. Accept my son's male lover? And, believe you me, he's had his share. When I first heard about this disease which is killing me—even before they called it AIDS—I just knew he'd get it. This had got to be God's punishment. And David flaunts his homosexuality. Openly queer. Why does he have to be open—especially now? I prayed, night after night, week after week, month after month, that God would forgive David and spare him. I could not live without his phone calls, his letters, his postcards, our valentine. My prayers have been answered. David does not show any signs of AIDS and I'm going to die from it. I ask myself, "Mary, what did you do to deserve this?" Am I being punished for my son's behavior? "You're turning him into a mama's boy." There were those nights, after I'd been out too late, drinking too much, when I'd come home and find David asleep in my bed. I'd try to wake him,

I'd try to move him. I knew it was wrong for a ten-year-old boy to sleep in the same bed with his mama. But his body made the bed warm. I was afraid to be alone and so was he. Sometimes I'd hold his hand—so little compared to his father's. Or the big, crusty hands of the men I'd meet at Blueskies, the neighborhood bar. David's hand was so soft in my hand. With my other hand, I'd stroke his baby fine blond hair which smelled of my favorite shampoo. One night I woke up to the sound of my own crying, startled, knowing his skin was pressed up against mine, holding me. Tight. Loving me. Part of me. This is my sin. Not his. AIDS is my punishment. I am ashamed. I deserve to die. God has given it to me and spared David. He has answered my prayers: there is a God! Holy Mary, mother of God. How will I tell David his mother deserves to die? Pray for us sinners. My heart hurts, missing my boy. My hands are empty, missing my boy. No matter how far apart, you beat in my heart. Now and at the hour of our death. Amen.

Phoenix

Phoenix is a homeless ex-con, black or Hispanic, fifties.

Yo, bro. My name is Phoenix—named after the city, not the bird. I've snorted MDA, swallowed LSD, shaken from the DTs and flown without the help of TWA. I tested positive for HIV and gone blind from CMV. That's right: I can't S-E-E. Now for the good news: I'm sixty-three days clean and sober. No shit, man. No fuckin' shit coursin' through my veins, bro. I been shootin' dope since I was a teenager. Learned how to in the joint. Learned how to do a lot of things in the joint. I been in and out of the pen for the past thirty years—mostly in. First time was for petty theft. Nothin' big time but I learned they treat ya better in there than they do out here on the street. Think about it: three meals a day, roof over your head, family. Got out this most recent time in '85. That was for armed robbery. I been livin' on the streets ever since. Got me a comfortable little abode right under the Hollywood Freeway. Bein' locked up doesn't exactly prepare you for a job. Can you imagine me at the B of fuckin' A? I pretty much been keepin' outta trouble. Beggin' for money instead stealin' it. Easier to beg now that I'm blind. Got a quarter, bro? Was shootin' dope even though I knew it was killin' me. About six months ago, I got a killer case of the shits. Which is pretty unfuckinusual for a junkie since weeks go by when I can't even take a shit. The diarrhea kept up—even though I was hardly eatin' a thing. Then I started losin' my vision. First one eye, then the other. I knew. I didn't need no doctor to tell me. I read the paper. I read the paper. Now I'm fuckin' blind with the fuckin' shits all the fuckin' time. That's the one nice thing about bein' homeless: when you gotta crap, you don't gotta run to the bathroom. A coupla months ago—sixty-five days to be exact—some young kid with a soft voice came to my abode and offered me a handful of syringes and some bleach. I'm real sensitive to voices since I can't fuckin' see. And smells. This kid smelled like a laundromat—clean. He musta been twenty or twenty-one years old. Sounded real educated. And a little superior. But gentle. Like I said: soft. Couldn't believe it when he tole me he was a drug addict. "I'm recovering," the kid said. "I'm a recovering drug addict with AIDS and while I'm alive, I want to stop spreading the disease." I tole him he was knockin' on my door a little bit late in the fuckin' day but thanks, anyway. Max came back the next day. I mean Luis. That's his name: Luis. I was all fucked up. Nasty. Shit in my pants. Foul. He said he wanted to take me to a meeting for drug addicts with AIDS. He smelled sweet. After he cleaned me up—that's when he tole me he was gay, somethin' I already kinda figured. Didn't make no difference to me. I was too sick and too tired to say no. He smelled like flowers. I don't remember much about that first meetin' 'cept they was all men. And their voices—some of them real masculine, others more soft, like Luis'—were filled with laughter. Alcoholics and drug addicts with AIDS—laughin' their butts off. Luis later tole me I was lucky I was blind 'cause I didn't have to see the expressions on their faces when he pranced me through the door. But, after a few days, they accepted me. Most of 'em. Tole me I was "chemically dependent"; I always thought I was a junkie. I call everybody "Bro." They like that. "Hey, bro, what's happenin'?" Luis gave me this cat, Max. We had a big fuckin' fight because I won't move from under the freeway. I went to the fuckin' clinic, wasn't that enough? No, he says, it's important for me to share a home. To touch somethin', someone. So he gave me Max, a cat without balls. Lives with me. Sometimes I call the cat "Luis" and I call Luis "Max." Might be the disease. Sometimes I pet Max and it's Luis' long, silky hair against my hands. Might be the disease. I been tryin' to kill myself for the past thirty years and it's finally gonna work. Godammit. The past sixty-three days have been a fuckin' miracle, man. I been loved, finally, by a queer boy and his cat. And I don't want to die. I want to love. I mean, live. Might be . . . But you know what? I'm ready, ready for . . . whatever. He smells like morning. He smells like rain. He smells like life.

more intimacies

Fernando

Fernando is a Hispanic flamenco dancer, fiftyish.

"A man needs to be fucked." Those were his exact words. This white boy with yellow hair, the color of corn. From Ohio. Or Iowa. I do not know the difference. "A man needs to be fucked." Jim. I call him Jim-Boy because he looks like he could have been on *The Waltons*. That's my children's favorite show; they watch all the reruns. Jim showed up at the club where I have been dancing for the past twenty-three years—since before he was born. He'd seen my picture in a newspaper advertisement. "I like manly men," he said to me. "Macho men, dark men, older men. Men with sturdy legs and strong stares." "I guess I fit the bill," I said to this boy with much guts, "but I am not gay." He did not blink. Those clear blue eyes stared right through me, penetrating me. "A man needs to be fucked," he whispered. Everyone assumes male dancers are queer. Not true! I grew up with kids taunting me. "Here comes the dancer," they'd say. As if dancer meant fairy, pansy, fruit. "Here comes the dancer." I learned to outrun them. Most of those guys are dead by now. Gang fights. I outran them and outlived them. Dancing was not what my father had in mind for his only son. "Dancing is for sissies," he'd hiss. In order to go to dancing school, I had to prove I was no sissy. I became a ladies' man at a very early age. My father was impressed—if not with my dancing ability, with my ability to attract beautiful girls. I got married to please my Dad. I was seventeen. Marrying Gabriella made it easier for my father to accept the idea of me becoming a dancer. There was never any question about what kind of dancer I'd be; from the time I was a little boy and saw a picture of a flamenco dancer, I knew. While other boys wanted to be Superman, I longed for the power and the passion I saw in that dancer's strong stare. His impenetrability. I tore that picture out of the book and carried it in my pocket. For inspiration. Thank God I was good enough to get a steady job, flamenco dancing, about the same time Gabriella got pregnant. After I moved away from home, I remember only two serious discussions with my father and both of them were about ass-fucking. One of these "man-to-man talks," as he called them, was when Gabriella ballooned up from the pregnancy. "You must not commit adultery," he said, being a strict Catholic. "Yet, being a man, you'll have urges and your wife will be too sick or too fat or too something," he said, looking me in the eye. "Find a boy, a puto, to fuck in the ass," he said, as if this was the Eleventh Commandment. "Find a puto to fuck in the ass. Feels great," he said. "You won't know the difference." Like Ohio and Iowa, I thought. So I did. And it did. Our second man-to-man talk came when Gabriella was pregnant with our third child, less than three years later. "You obviously haven't figured out how to practice birth control," he said. I knew he wasn't talking about rubbers, forbidden by the Church. "You must learn to fuck her like you fuck those pretty boy putos. Then no more babies." Suddenly I knew why I was an only child. Gabriella wouldn't go for it—"hurt too bad," she said—so we had two more kids in as many years. Five hungry kids to feed on the salary of a flamenco dancer was not easy. Many women at the club had offered me gifts. And I accepted. I knew they wanted to feel what was between the flamenco dancer's sturdy legs. When a lady presented me with a hundred dollar bill, I knew she wanted more than a feel. I blamed Gabriella. If she'd let me do what my father suggested, I wouldn't need to fuck this old bag for a hundred bucks. But I did; the kids needed to eat. It became a weekly ritual with this rich old broad. Then I started servicing her girlfriends. I was exhausted but I was making an extra thousand dollars a month. That was fifteen years ago. I still—even at my age—get offers. As long as they don't see my feet, I can make a few extra bucks. As long as it doesn't spread up my legs. Onto my face. Into my mouth. There's one conversation my father and I did not have about butt-fucking. A conversation that might have saved my life. "A man needs to be fucked," Jim-Boy said. He's rubbing my feet. We're in his hotel room, which he's rented for the weekend. The picture of me in the newspaper advertisement is on the dresser. "You have so much attitude when you're on stage," he says. I don't understand "attitude." "Charisma," he says. "Oh! Garbo is what you're meaning." "Garbo? Like in Greta Garbo?" he asks. We laugh. He begins licking my feet, putting each toe in his mouth, like they are cherry Popsicles. Sucking my toes. I am feeling things I have never felt before. He tickles my feet with his silky yellow hair; I feel his finger slide into my ass as he works his way up from my feet, kissing my ankles, my calves, my knees, my thighs, my balls. I am completely wet. His tongue is inside me. I will never be the same. He fucks me with his tongue and then he's on top of me, kissing my face, whispering in my ear. "Tell me how much you need it," he says. "Tell me how much you need it." "I need to be fucked," I hear myself say, under the spell of this boy from Iowa. Or Ohio. It does not hurt but I feel tears on my face. Or could it be the juices from his mouth? I am coming. I am gay! I am not gay! I am a husband and a father. A good Catholic. I am a Spanish flamenco dancer. I am not Mexican. I am a ladies' man. Those are not lesions on my feet. They are badges of passion, purple tattoos oozing from places on my skin where his lips touched, feet first, then moving up my legs, inside my ass, up my chest, inside my mouth, until I am covered with his lovely kisses, his deadly marks. A violet shroud of love and death. I will not die. He gave me his youth. Injected me with immortality. Into my brain. I do not have AIDS. I am not gay. I am not a grandfather. I am impenetrable. Superman. Immortal. Spanish, not Mexican. A ladies' man. A man needs to be fucked. I am a ladies' man who needs to be fucked. Now I know the difference. Before Jim-Boy I did not know the difference. Between straight and gay. Life and death, Ohio and Iowa. Now I know. The truth.

Jesse

Jesse is a middle-aged black lesbian junkie.

This here dyke don't hate men. I hate dick. I got them three words tattooed on my left arm: "I hate dick." You ain't never seen a black broad with a tattoo? This one's got two. The one on my right arm says, "Mom." Readin' those tattoos is like readin' chapters of my life. The track marks is the Table of Contents. But nobody's gonna read me today. Curtain is closed. Long sleeve shirt is hidin' all clues leadin' to Jesse's true story. A mournful story of love and hate, the kind sung by a drugged-up diva. I grew up listenin' to them bluesy mamas singin' from their bleedin', gin-soaked guts. Every time my mama'd get shit on by a man, she'd listen to Bessie or Billie and cry her eyes out. In bed. She was always in bed—either gettin' fucked or gettin' over gettin' fucked. The only time she got dressed up was to go find another man and that didn't take long 'cause she was a beauty—even at the end. These men were all alike. She'd force me to call 'em "Daddy" whether they was there for an hour or a month. My real Daddy was as foreign to me as the king of fuckin' Siam. These men were a bunch of dicks, always leavin' her. She'd lie on that bed, sheets smellin' of sex and cigarette smoke and Scotch. She'd turn her records up full volume and wail along like she was a tortured star. Which she was. I became the man of the house by necessity. I took care of her day and night. Sometimes these motherfuckers would give us money; some-times I'd pick their pockets after they passed out. I'd do odd jobs to make money—passed myself off as a boy to mow lawns. Then I got a steady job workin' for a white lady who ran a laundry. Part of the deal was I got to wash mama's

31

sheets for free. But I had to hide from the customers 'cause they wouldn't want to think their lily white linens had been folded by colored hands. That's what we was then: "colored." One day—when I was twelve or thirteen—I came home from the laundry and found mama dead. Fresh blood all over one of them snow white sheets I'd scrubbed and folded myself. With my colored hands. Billie was singin' on the Victrola. Mama'd slashed her wrists. Over a dick. That's when I vowed never to let a dick ruin my life. That's also about the time when I got my "Mom" tattoo—"Mom" written on the inside of a bleedin' heart. I went and lived with my grandma who forced me to wear a dress to school. I hated her for it. I knew what I wanted to be, what I wanted to wear. I discovered my first lez bar before I was old enough to drink—a bar where half the women wore dresses and the other half of us dressed like men. Fuck Grandma! This was the fifties; walkin' up to that bar, we was passin'. On account of the fuckin' police. This bar I'm tellin' you about was my salvation. It was a jazz club with an all-female jazz band. One night I got up to sing—"God Bless The Child"—and the place went wild. I was jus' imitatin' those records I heard all my life. But I learned how to sing. I also learned how to shoot up. One night when we was high, I got me my second tattoo. "I hate dick." Even though I walked like a man, talked like a man, dressed like a man, and sang like a man—there was always some dick who thought he could change you. I'd show 'em my arm, track marks and tattoo, which I never bothered cov-erin' up in those days. Now that I manage this apartment building, I have to play the game. Hide my habits. I been managin' this building for about fifteen years. Although I'm not supposed to discriminate, I do: Womens only. With one exception: this sorry ass deaf and dumb dude I rented to a coupla years ago. I figured he'd be nice and quiet and wouldn't be complainin' about the broads' noise—bitch fights and butch fights and cat fights and bull fights. This kid—I think he's a fairy, but I ain't seen nobody visitin' him—keeps to hisself. Me too, since my marriage died. Literally. Miss Jill. What's known as a lipstick lesbian. Femme fatal—all dolled up like one of them Charlie's Angels. A drunk. Now I'm one of those tough motherfuckers who can handle drugs and shit. Some people liven up their weekend with hot dogs. Or Haagen Daz. I prefer heroin. But I know when to stop. Miss Jill had a problem with booze 'n shit. Didn't know when to stop. I stopped givin' her money but she kept comin' home pissed to the tits. Nice tits, by the way. We was husband and wife for two years. I wore the pants in the family. During the last year, she spent mosta her time in bed. Sick as a bitch. At night, she'd sweat like a motherfucker. I'd change the sheets every morning. Thank God this building's got a laundry room. She was always a skinny chick—weighed about half a what I do—but she started lookin' like a skeleton. I couldn't stand seein' her shrivel up and die. I started shootin' up—but only days endin' in "y." Miss Jill never shot up; she was your garden variety alkie. She said she was afraid of catchin' AIDS by shootin' drugs. I tole her I shared needles with people I wouldn't drink outta the same glass with and I ain't caught no fuckin' disease. Dick is what carries AIDS, baby: that's what I tole her. Turns out I was right. Jill died of AIDS. Finally admitted she was gettin' butt-fucked to pay for her booze. She thought only queers could get AIDS up the ass, she said on her deathbed. Everybody in the building—includin' that faggot deaf mute—heard me screamin' the night she tole me. I hate dick. Some dick is killin' my gal. It was an ugly death. This time I had to burn the sheets. I started losin' weight about a month later. Thought it was because of the death. Diarrhea all the time. Thought it was the drugs. Sweatin' all night long like my mama did—I mean, like Jill did. I looked in the mirror one day and I realized I was wastin' away to nothin'. Then I figured it out: that dick had infected me through Jill. Dicks have been tryin' to destroy me my entire fuckin' life. This dick did the trick. I needed to talk to someone. I needed to tell someone I was dyin'. But I didn't want no fuckin' lectures. I just wanted someone to listen; someone who wouldn't talk back. I knocked on his door—hard as I could. I musta pounded on that door for half an hour. I knew he was in there. Finally, I used my master key and let myself in. I musta scared the shit outta him. He looked pissed off at first. I didn't say a word. We was like two animals, just sensin' each other. He could probably smell death all over me. All of a sudden, this weird, sweet smile came over his face and he opened his arms. Nobody in my life has ever understood my pain. Next thing I knew, I was bein' held by a deaf and dumb dick. A dick. And I was cryin'. Then singin'. And he was rockin' me, cradlin' me in his arms while I sang.

Father Anthony

Father Anthony is a Roman Catholic priest, 35 to 45.

We were not identical twins—not identical in any way. Even as kids, my mama says, we were as different as day and night, black and white. For one thing, Vinnie has—*had*—this bright red hair, from the time he was a baby. A red-headed Italian. My hair's always been black—like the rest of the family. Vinnie was this rambunctious kid, always overactive. I remember he broke something three summers in a row. His arm. His collarbone. His wrist. He wasn't athletic as much as he was physical: climbing trees, bike-riding in the pouring rain, showing off on the monkey bars. He drove our folks crazy with hospital bills. I was the opposite of Vinnie. Even our names, Vincent and Anthony. How's that for two Italian Catholic boys from New York? Nobody ever called me Tony. Ever. To this day. But he was always Vinnie; nobody ever called him Vincent. I was always the good boy—serious, studious, determined to make our parents proud. When I went into the seminary, Vinnie enrolled in Cosmetology School. I swear he did it just to infuriate our parents, especially our father. A hairdresser! I stayed close to home while Vinnie traveled all over the world: London, Paris, Los Angeles. We lost touch with him. Then, one Sunday evening a couple of years ago, I was visiting my parents—I have dinner with my folks every Sunday night—and this news segment came on TV. Something about Gay Pride Day in San Francisco. And there was Vinnie: red hair and all, bigger than life, in a parade. Twirling a baton! My parents became hysterical. Lots of tears from my mom and shouting from my father. They decided to disown him. There were lots of AIDS victims in the parade and I remember my father saying it was God's will. The following Sunday in church, my sermon upheld the teachings of the Catholic church: Homosexuality is not condoned; there is no such thing as safe sex; abstinence is the answer. At least my parents had one son to be proud of. I was shocked to hear from Vinnie about a year later. We had hardly spoken during our entire adult life. He had two tickets to go to Paris, he said, and he wanted to take his twin brother. I don't know why, but—without telling my parents—I went. The first night there, we went to this elegant restaurant: Dodin Bouffant. Vinnie chose it—partly because of the name, a hair reference. "Bouffant as in girl singers from the fifties," he said. He could be very funny. There was a beautiful woman at the table across from us who mesmerized me. I guess you could say she was a free spirit. She was flirting with an older bald man—kissing him on his shiny, smooth head, running her long red fingernails along his neck. Very sexy. Seductive. When she stood up to leave, I got a look at her long black skirt, slit all the way up, revealing these incredible legs. She was so uninhibited, so comfortable with herself. So passionate. She reminded me of Vinnie. The next day we went to the Louvre and saw the David show. There was a woman, being yanked away from the exhibit by her crude husband. "You've seen enough," he said. Determined to please him, she left, looking longingly over her shoulder at those dramatic, sensual masterpieces. She was wearing a blouse, buttoned to her neck, strangling her. She looked constipated. Squelched. I saw myself in her. Those two women were as different as Vinnie and me. The Paris trip didn't make sense to me until I got word, about six months later, that my brother was in the hospital and would probably not leave. Again, unbeknownst to my parents, I went to his side. I'll say this: He never lost his sense of humor. He was shaving one day—he insisted on shaving himself even though he was terribly weak—and he dropped the hand mirror. It shattered. There was a pause. "In my case, that's seven days' bad luck," he said. He died eight days later. He'd lost all his beautiful red hair. I've been a priest for almost ten years and being with my brother when he died is the only spiritual experience I've ever known: I kissed his bald head and caressed his neck with my fingertips. After he died, I told him a secret: "We are identical," I said. "I have AIDS, too." I did not get infected from handling my brother's shit; I did not get infected from wiping my brother's tears; I did not get infected from touching my brother's vomit; I did not get infected from tasting my brother's saliva. I loved his puke. I loved his diarrhea. I loved his sweat and I loved his spit and I loved his tears. I got infected from having sex with boys in my parish, hustlers off the street, husbands of wives who come to me for marriage counseling. Being a good Catholic, I didn't use a condom. Neither did they. Even a disposable condom was too much evidence for Father Anthony. Not only have I—in the name of Holy Mother, the church—killed my own twin brother, I've murdered all my brothers. How many Hail Marys should I say for penance? Perhaps I should splatter, not red paint, but my own blood on the steps of the Vatican. Perhaps I should pin a pink triangle on my long black skirt. Perhaps I should learn how to love my fellow man. If it weren't for my parents. They're in their seventies. It would kill them. I'm all they have. Father Anthony is all they have. If there is a merciful God—which I doubt—surely he will take them before me.

Mike

Mike is a redneck hemophiliac, fortyish.

My mama always tole me that boys with hemophilia had three things in common: we was bright; we was good lookin'; we was all daredevils. My name is Mike. I'm an alcoholic. And a daredevil. My brain cells and my looks are ancient history, but I'm still a fuckin' daredevil. Or I wouldn't be here. I been called a lot of other things—from "Mama's boy" to "motherfucker." When I was a kid, I was called a "sissy" because I couldn't do sports. On account of the danger. I had to be real careful: bleedin'. In gym class I was graded on how I'd put the equipment away and take the roll call. My fuckin' mother wouldn't let me out of her sight. She was always guilt-trippin' herself about me. "It's all my fault," she'd piss and moan. "It's all my fault." Drove my old man fuckin' nuts. She never paid no attention to the poor bastard so he eventually split. That's when she really started drinkin'. That's when I started drinkin'. If I did have an accident—even a bump against a piece of furniture could cause internal bleedin'—it'd be real painful. She began medicatin' me with a few sips from her drink. Tasted good. Then she started pourin' me a drink whenever she poured herself one. Which was pretty fuckin' often. By the time I was in high school, I had learned to out drink her. After she'd pass out, I'd go out and get into some trouble. Drunk on my butt. Lots of times I'd hurt myself and wind up in the Emergency Room for a blood transfusion. She'd come rescue me, hysterical. "You're all I've got," she'd say. "It's my fault." I started hatin' her. I started stayin' out all night. When I'd come home the next mornin', she'd be in a panic. Drinkin', wringin' her hands. When I got me a girl,

Jeaneanne, she became insanely jealous. Insane. She was either beggin' me to stay home or threatenin' to kick me outta the house. I got Jeaneanne pregnant! Proved I was no sissy! I decided to marry her. For one thing, it would get me out of the house, get me away from that hysterical, drunken, smothering bitch. Jeaneanne had a boy. A healthy boy! He was normal; he would have a normal childhood—somethin' I never knew. Jeaneanne started givin' him a bunch of attention. "I got two little boys to take care of," she always liked to say. It's true, she did take care of me. I didn't work, couldn't hold down a job. I was drinkin' pretty heavy and startin' in with motorcycles. Motorcycles got me outta the house, away from Jeaneanne and Little Mike. I was only happy when I was on a bike, stoned outta my mind, on my way somewhere. Nowhere. I had a bunch of accidents and wound up in the Emergency Room. By this time, we bleeders had this blood concentrate shit which made life easier. But I had already begun gettin' arthritis from bleedin' in my joints and was in chronic pain. Motorcycle wrecks didn't help none. Had to have a shoulder replacement. And a knee replacement. Jeaneanne raised Little Mike pretty much by herself. He was a tough little bastard. By the time he was a teenager, he really fuckin' hated me. One night I had this gigantic blowout with Jeaneanne. I was drunk outta my mind and I guess I hit her pretty bad. Well, Little Mike freaked out and almost killed me. Seriously. Missed my face and punched me in the neck. Started bleedin' internally, in my throat, and couldn't breathe. Can't say I blame him; I asked for it. That's when he forced her to choose. Between him and me. She said she couldn't make the decision so he made it for her. He split. More than ten years ago. That's when we hemophiliacs started hearin' about AIDS—a disease for faggots and drug addicts, spread by butt-fuckin' and needle sharin'. They warned us that the concentrate may have been polluted by these fuckin' degenerates so a bunch of hemophiliacs started gettin' the AIDS test. Not me! No fuckin' way was I gonna volunteer to go to a fuckin' doctor's office. I spent my life goin' to the doctor. I survived this far; no fag disease was gonna kill me. Only bad people got AIDS. I thought if a hemophiliac got it, he must be a secret cocksucker or fuckin' axe murderer. Jeaneanne tried to get me to wear a fuckin' rubber—like some scared sissy. "I'm not the pussy—you are," I'd tell her. "And if you don't let me fuck you without a faggot rubber, I'll find some broad who will." And I did—plenty of 'em. Jeaneanne had enough of my shit and started goin' to meetings for wives of alcoholics or some such bullshit. "Shouldn't I be the one goin' to meetings?" I asked her. She seemed to be gettin' happier while I was gettin' sicker. The booze wouldn't even kill the pain. I was exhausted, constantly sick and tired. I couldn't ride my bike—fuck, I couldn't walk across the room. She'd be at her meetings while I'd be at home, burnin' up with fever and shittin' in my pants. One night I had to call my ole lady to come over and clean me up. "My baby," she kept sayin' over and over again, like she was thrilled shitless I was covered in crap. "It's all my fault." Jeaneanne took care of me less and less but she agreed to take me to get the AIDS test. The doctor took one look at me and knew. I jus' couldn't believe it. What was I bein' punished for? Jeaneanne started laughin' when I said that. Laughin' in my face. I remember—barely, 'cause I was drunk at the time—grabbin' a knife and goin' for her throat. To stop the laughter. People been laughin' at me my entire fuckin' life. She knew it was time to kick my ass out for real. After more than twenty years. I had nowhere to go but home to my pathetic ole lady. That was the worst moment of my entire, miserable, fucked-up life. Rock bottom. I began to pray: "Let me die quick." Started thinkin' about slashin' my wrists. Losin' blood didn't scare me. Bleedin' to death is what I been doin' all my fuckin' life. Found out that Little Mike came home to see Jeaneanne. I wanted to see him before I fuckin' did myself in. "He won't see you if you're drunk," Jeaneanne said when I called her. "Then I'll get sober," I said. Simple as that. "I dare you," she said. I tole you I'm still a daredevil. Jeaneanne gave me a number to call and I been sober for twenty-five days. Livin' in a halfway house, away from my poor old lady. Got together a coupla weeks ago with Little Mike (who is bigger than I am). He's queer. That's what he tole me. Gay! "Jesusfuckingchrist, is it my fault?" He says it ain't; he was born that way, he says, like I was born hemophiliac. It's natural to him; he likes bein' different. I asked him if he caught AIDS yet. He says he don't have sex. "Then how you know you're gay?" I ask. He just laughed. But not at me. I laughed, too. For the first time in years and fuckin' years. I guess I gotta lot to learn.

Deede

Deede is a pregnant yuppie, thirty something.

His final three words to me were "I love you." I'm lying. His final three words were sprayed on the mirror of the guest bedroom with that stuff that makes snow on Christmas windows. It was big, flowing, white snowy letters: "I HAVE AIDS." Those were his final three words. "I have AIDS." Not "I have AIDS, I'm gay." Just "I have AIDS." Why didn't he tell me? I've been around gay guys all my life; there's never a time when they weren't around. My mother loves gay men. When I was a little girl, I called them my uncles. Some of them would call themselves my aunts. As a kid, I never thought about what they did in bed. It was presented to me as natural so it came as a big shock to me to learn that homosexuals were not considered normal by every family on the block. I wound up going to art school where, again, gays were pretty much the norm. I got into interior design—a friend of Mom's, naturally. I stared doing massage back in '83. I was 24. A virgin. Can you believe it? I was. And Don was a client. He was in the midst of a heavy-duty divorce. Stressed to the max. He had these knots in his neck and shoulders, like rocks. After a few sessions, he started to relax. He asked me out. We fell in love. But I wouldn't have sex with him until after his divorce was final. I'd waited that long! It's funny when I think about it. My girlfriends were always joking that I, at least, would never come down with AIDS. A lot of my mother's friends were getting sick around this time. I massaged some of them. It was scary at first but I knew there was no chance of catching it. Don never objected to me working on these guys with AIDS. That really endeared him to me.

When I think back, there were probably clues. But I'd never had a fulfilled sexual relationship with anyone. Even after his divorce, we didn't have sex. He didn't want to; he said he was recovering. We made out—lots. When we finally did do it, it wasn't what I'd anticipated. What I'm trying to say is that he didn't like to have intercourse as much as he liked me to go down on him. According to most of my girlfriends, that's not so unusual. A coupla years ago, we started watching porno videos during sex. I used to pick them up at the video store next to the grocery store. It was just like selecting another flavor of soup. But one day I picked up a tape—without paying much attention, I guess—with two guys in it. Two guys and a woman. *Bi and Beyond.* I'll never forget watching that tape, lying there in bed with Don, and these two guys start going at it. I apologized and said I'd made a mistake. "It's all right, honey," he said. Well, we had great sex. I honestly think that's the night I conceived. We must have done it—I mean "it"—four or five times. At the time, I didn't think much about it. We went back to straight movies and he never mentioned it again. I found out I was pregnant a coupla months later. Due around Christmas. This made Don ecstatic. He had this lousy childhood—never knew what it was like to celebrate the holidays. So having a baby on Christmas was making him hysterically happy. *It's a Wonderful Life* is his favorite film. I'm not kidding. As I got more pregnant, *It's a Wonderful Life* replaced the porn movies. He watched it until he knew every word by heart; he could recite the entire movie. It was a rough pregnancy. I was sick a lot. Then Don started getting sick. Someone suggested it was sympathetic illness. He had the flu. Started around Thanksgiving. I remember when we got the Christmas tree, he could barely carry it to and from the car. I was gaining weight and he was losing. He refused to go to the doctor. A month-long flu where we live is not unusual. He stopped working and turned our guest bedroom into a Christmas fantasy. There was an electric train, dozens of beautifully wrapped presents for me and the baby, and a video of *It's a Wonderful Life* playing around the clock. We live on the thirty-seventh floor. Sometimes the wind was so fierce, it would cause the Christmas tree to sway back and forth. Beautiful. He loved that. He looked out the window and talked about the power of the wind. He seemed feverish at times. He'd wake me in the night, sweating. He knew I needed my sleep so he began sleeping in the Christmas room where I imagine he was very happy. By the time Christmas arrived, he couldn't get out of bed. No baby yet. I'm two weeks overdue now. We celebrated. Tried to. He was very groggy. The morning after Christmas, I went in to check on him. He seemed a little better. I brought him some orange juice and he drank a coupla sips. "I love you," he said. And he patted my stomach. He asked me to turn up the volume on *It's a Wonderful Life*. I went back to sleep in the other room. The next thing I heard was pounding at the front door. It was two policemen. "Do you know Don Swerling?" one of them asked. I didn't even answer—I ran into the Christmas room. The window was wide open. The only comfort I've had is in watching that porn video. *Bi and Beyond.* Two guys and a woman. When I think back, that's probably the most honest he ever was with me. I watch those two guys—one blond and one brunette—and I fantasize he's one or the other of them. He's the blond one getting screwed from behind. He's the dark one getting sucked. He's being kissed, licked—his neck, his nipples, his face, his feet. He's being loved. And I'm watching. Not judging him. Just accepting him. As he is. Was. I watch that movie, over and over and over. Two men having sex. It's okay. If only he'd told me.

Paul

Paul is a hearing-impaired young man, mid thirties.

(On tape in "normal" voice) I remember screaming. What it was like to scream. To cry. To express myself. I remember the sound. The sound of my voice. Screaming. Crying. I remember the sound of his voice, screaming. And the sound of her voice, crying. I do not remember the sound of laughter. Or "coochy-coochy-coo." I do not remember hearing "I love you." I do not remember hearing my name. Paul is my name. I have been deaf all my life, almost. Since I was five years old. "High fever," is what they told me. Two words: high fever. Like high school, high tide, high noon, high hopes. That was the explanation: high fever. I do not remember laughing. Or hoping. No hope. No high hopes. No sound. No voice. No more screams, no more cries. I knew I did something wrong; I knew I was bad. It was all my fault. Even though I couldn't hear, I knew he was screaming at me. And she was crying because of me. It was all my fault. I could not hear. I could not speak. I was bad. I was a freak. They sent me to a normal school with hearing kids. I was not really deaf, they insisted, I would get over it. I was forbidden to learn sign language. I attempted to read lips. I only knew one other deaf person my age, a boy I was forbidden to see. I met him accidentally in a park; he was there with his parents, who were also deaf. They were a happy family, speaking sign language. "They look like animals in the zoo," my father said. Scott was his name and he'd come to my house when my parents were not home. He taught me how to sign. He taught me how to jack off. We were ten or eleven. He taught me to speak with my hands and fingers: "Feels great," he'd say, putting my hands on his cock and balls. Then he'd put

his hands on mine and I'd sign, "Feels great." He taught me to speak without words, with my tongue and my mouth. He stuck his tongue inside my ear and for a moment I thought I heard the words "I love you." He spoke with his tongue and his fingertips. "Feels great," I'd sign, a good student. My father caught us, in bed, naked. We'd fallen asleep in each other's arms with our worn-out fingers entwined. My father beat the shit out of me and told Scott's parents—wrote them, actually—about their "deaf and dumb faggot of a son." I went to sleep that night smelling Scott on my sheets and tasting blood in my mouth. The message was clear: The only thing worse than being deaf was being a fag. *(Live in deaf accent)* I learned to speak to please my Dad. I got married to please my Dad. To a hearing girl, naturally. It was a disaster. I could not fuck any better than I could speak. Once in a while, remembering Scott's soft, wet tongue in my ear, I could perform. But mostly I'd fail. She thought it was because I was deaf; I guess she thought all deaf guys are impotent. Don't laugh. Most people think we can't drive a car. I began—secretly, of course—pursuing men. In the park. In public johns. Anonymous encounters where I didn't have to speak. I gave new meaning to playing hard-to-get. Guys would ask me my name, I wouldn't respond. Guys would ask me what I liked to do, I wouldn't respond. Remember, this was the seventies. They didn't think I was deaf, they though I was hot. I became a star of the Anonymous Sex Circuit. A silent star but a compulsive one who never once even said "thank you." I divorced my wife, much to the dismay of my parents. I divorced my parents. I isolated, collecting SSI and trying to fit in by reading books about hearing people and watching movies about straight people. Sex was my only human contact. On bodies of nameless strangers, I composed love songs with my tongue, wrote sonnets with my fingertips. And I could do it all—fuck, get fucked, suck, get sucked, you name it—standing up. Just don't ask me to talk dirty. I didn't consider myself gay, any more than I considered myself deaf. I thought you had to go to bed—to a man's bedroom—to be gay, to get AIDS. I began getting mysterious ailments in 1986 or '87. I went to the Free Clinic. They tested me. Two weeks later—after daily unsafe and unsound encounters against cold white porcelain and under dying dry brown branches—I got the results. Positive. "There is an available counselor who knows how to sign," the doctor wrote, under the word "Positive." He also handed me a pamphlet: AIDS and the Deaf. I ripped up the pamphlet and stormed out of the clinic, realizing for the first time in my life: I am gay, I am deaf, and I'm going to die. Alone. No friends, no family, no one to tell. No way to tell. Nothing. Suicide. I could blow my brains out without hearing a thing. Instead, I went back to the clinic to find that pamphlet, AIDS and the Deaf. I went to this meeting. There was a room filled with gay, deaf men, using sign language, communicating passionately. They were all infected with HIV. We sat in a circle and everyone told his story—in sign. Even though I didn't fully understand, I got enough. What I didn't get, this really cute guy wrote down for me. When my turn came, thank God I remembered those words Scott had taught me to sign: "Feels great." Gradually, I began to get honest with myself. *(Live in deaf accent, accompanied by signing)* I finally learned to sign. I finally admitted what I've known all along: my deafness was not caused by a high fever. My father had beaten me into silence. "It doesn't matter how," this guy in the group says. "Deafness is a gift." He also believes being gay is a gift. And having HIV is a gift. His name is Billy. He describes himself as part Helen Keller and part Mary Poppins. He's the opposite of me. But I love him. Except for Scott, Billy is the only person I've ever had sex with in a horizontal position. The only person I've ever made love with— that's a gift. For sure. *(Sign only)* Feels great!

ROCK

Rocky

Rocky is an innocent from Little Rock, transplanted to Los Angeles, twenties.

The day Rock Hudson died, I got my cherry popped in the Greyhound Bus Station on Vine Street near Sunset Boulevard. This guy, who looked like he coulda been a movie star himself, insisted on putting not one, but two, rubbers on. I'll never forget that.

My Mama was already on the bus, which was headin' home to Little Rock, when I realized I had to take a shit. The bus driver said I had exactly five minutes which woulda been plenty of time to take a dump—if I hadn't met Frank. (Actually, I didn't meet him until a year later; if I hadn't gotten fucked by Frank.)

I was sitting on the toilet, wiping myself, with about two and a half minutes to spare when this big, handsome guy bursts into that tiny little crapper. First thing he did was touched my hair, just kinda ran his fingers through my hair. It was the first time a man had ever touched me. Ever. I thought I was gonna cry. I didn't know what had hit me. Then he kissed my forehead. I remember the feeling of his beard—he had a stubble—scratching against my cheek. I stood up and he started strokin' my ass, rubbin' his hands up and down my backside. I can't remember if he turned me around or if I just volunteered but next thing I knew, he was putting not one, but two, rubbers on his big, hard dick. My cock was as hard as it had ever been in my entire fuckin' life. Rock hard.

Right as he began stickin' it in (he'd put some sticky stuff on it—this guy was prepared), I heard my Mama screamin',

51

"Rock! The bus is leavin'. Rock, can you hear me? You're gonna miss the bus! Rock!"

I could hear the engine of the bus, outside the window of the john, revvin' up. He's squeezin' my nipples, his cock is inside me, beginning to slide in and out. "Rock! Am I gonna have to come in there and get you?"

Now she's poundin' on the door as his body is poundin' up against me. For the first time in my life, I decide I'm not gonna let that fucking bitch destroy my happiness. Not this time.

The bus driver starts honkin' and I hear her scream, "I'm leavin' without you, you little prick." My prick was anything but little. He is kissing my ear. "I'm gonna give it to you, Rocky," he whispered. I swear, it was so hot in my butt I could smell rubber burnin' mixed with the piss and shit smells of the john. And the smell of his hot breath on my neck and in my ear.

The noisy bus was pullin' away, drownin' out the sound of him gruntin' as he came inside me and I, no longer a virgin, shot my wad all over the wall of the Hollywood Greyhound bus station. That was October 2, 1985. That day changed my life. For one thing, I came out—after 26 years of tryin' to be straight, tryin' to please that ravin' bitch. It's also the day I changed my name. To Rocky. That's what Frank called me ("I'm gonna give it to you, Rocky").

I was named after Rock Hudson. My mama was in love with Rock Hudson, obsessed with Rock Hudson, the way some women are obsessed with Elvis. There were pictures of Rock Hudson on every square inch of the trailer we lived in: movie magazines, newspaper articles, autographed pictures.

She measured time by events in Rock Hudson's life: she married my father the year Rock did *Giant;* I was born the year he did *Pillow Talk;* my father disappeared the year he did *Lover Come Back.*

"Disappeared." That's the only word she ever used to describe my father: "disappeared." I'm not sure she even knew his name. She mighta made him up—like a lot of other things.

She changed her name to Doris and bleached her hair blond the year he did *Send Me No Flowers*, his third movie with Doris Day. I was about five. She made me call her "Doris" instead of "Mom" or "Mommy." So I had "Doris" for a mother and "Disappeared" for a father.

Our life revolved around Rock Hudson. "You are gonna grow up to be just like Rock Hudson," she'd always say. Of course, I was a little sissy. She used to force me to watch him on *McMillan and Wife* and then she'd make me imitate him. Here I was, this thirteen-year-old kid, trying to walk and talk like Rock Hudson. She'd spend hours, getting me to lower my voice and swagger across the room. But the minute she'd turn her back, I'd put on her Doris Day records and lip-sync to "Que Sera, Sera."

We lived in this trailer park and except when I went to school, she would not let me out of her sight. I guess she was afraid I'd disappear, like my Dad.

After I'd graduated from high school and began working at the local post office, she really got crazy. Crazier. When someone told her that Rock Hudson was queer, she became insane, trying to convince me Rock Hudson was my father. I began to wonder if he was my father. Or a queer. Or both. I figured maybe that's why I was a queer. I mean, I knew watchin' Rock Hudson and other men on TV gave me a boner. I'd hide in the john and beat off, thinking about those TV stars fucking me in the butt. But all I did was think about it—until that day in Hollywood.

When she heard that Rock Hudson had open heart surgery, while he was filming *The Devlin Connection*, I thought she was gonna have a heart attack. She made all these elaborate get well cards which I'd mail to him at Cedars-Sinai in West Hollywood. She'd sign them, "Doris of Little Rock," and she'd include all these bullshit religious quotes.

A few years later, when a sickly-looking picture of Rock—with Nancy and Ronnie Reagan!—showed up in our local paper, she became frantic. When she saw how skinny he was on *Dynasty,* she started sendin' him cakes and cookies and pies which I'd mail from the post office. Of course, she had his home address. Don't ask how she got it. If that crazy bitch taught me anything, it's that you can get whatever you want in this world. From the moment it came on the news that Rock Hudson had AIDS, she insisted, "He's a real man; Rock got it from a blood transfusion when he had that heart attack." She began makin' plans to go to Hollywood, sellin' everything we owned—she even sold a couple of autographed pictures of Rock—in order to buy two bus tickets to California.

We rode across the country and arrived at the bus station in the wee hours of the mornin' on October 1 and then got a cab to his house. "The Castle," they called it. We stood by the gate until the sun came up; she didn't want to disturb his sleep. She was prayin' constantly—sometimes speaking in tongues.

At about 7:00 A.M., she rang the bell and spoke to someone who told her to go away. She said she wouldn't leave until she saw Rock Hudson; God had sent her to heal him. We stayed there all day. People came and went. A few reporters said he was in a coma.

That night, this middle-aged queen came out from the house and invited my mother in. He told her that Pat Boone and his wife were coming over to pray for Rock—Pat Boone and his wife!—and she could come in, too. I said I'd wait outside.

She came out about a half an hour later, and told me that Pat Boone had anointed Rock. After that, she said, Rock opened his eyes and prayed with her. He held her hands but he couldn't talk. His face was "glowing," she said. She was ready to go back to Little Rock.

We got a motel room in Hollywood, near the bus station, and slept until about noon the next day. Right before we left for the bus station, a news break interrupted the soap opera she was watchin': "Hollywood legend Rock Hudson, dead of

AIDS at age 60." She didn't say a word. Not a word. Doris was silent. In fact—except for when she was screechin' outside the toilet door—I've never heard her voice since. Or seen her face, for that matter.

Later that evening, I found a wadded $20 bill and a wrinkled piece of paper with Frank's name and phone number on it; he musta slipped it into my pocket (after he slipped it to me). With that extra $20, I had enough money to spend the night at a motel. I watched the news. There was this slimy old queen, bein' interviewed, who said that Rock Hudson died of "anorexia nervosa." Then there was this other guy sayin' that Rock Hudson died of "Hollywood homophobia in addition to complications from AIDS."

I fell in love with Hollywood. And I fell in love in Hollywood—with lots of guys, all shapes and sizes and colors. I made up for lost time. But I was real careful—always wore two rubbers (or insisted the other guy did). I got a waiter job. An apartment. Some clothes. A car—used, of course. I even took some acting classes. You'd be amazed how quickly I became your run-of-the-mill gay boy.

I never called Frank but I never threw away that wrinkled piece of paper with his phone number. I'd thrown away dozens of numbers but never his. His was special. It's kinda weird but Rock Hudson was special to me, too. So I began takin' care of his star on Hollywood Boulevard. Nobody else did. I'd go up there and polish it once a week. Sometimes people would make comments. Even other queers seemed to hate him. But I felt indebted to him. If it weren't for him, I might still be in Little Rock, trying to be straight.

A year after Hudson died, I decided to call Frank. It was my one year anniversary as a queer: October 2, 1986. He answered the phone on the first ring—very unusual for a gay guy in Los Angeles.

I couldn't believe it but he remembered me. I asked him if I could come over. To celebrate. He was hesitant, but then he said I could.

I didn't recognize Frank when he opened the door. He was real skinny and had all the signs: lesions, grayish skin, no hair. I wanted to run at first but then I just wanted to hold him. So I did. I held him. For hours.

Up to this point, I'd had a lot of dates/tricks/affairs but I'd never really had a Relationship. The first thing he insisted was that I get tested (I'm negative) and he made me promise, over and over and over again, that I'd take care of myself.

I wound up moving in with Frank, in order to take care of him. It just seemed natural. We didn't have sex but I guess you could say we were lovers. Because we did make love—not in the sexual way but in other ways. Ways I can't describe. He stayed alive for two more years. Because of me, he always said. He died in 1988. In my arms.

I still take care of Rock's star on the Boulevard. Every Sunday morning. It's a ritual. When I'm through, I visit Frank's grave at Hollywood Memorial. He wanted to be buried near Valentino—another queer movie star.

Sometimes I'll be walkin' down the street, or drivin' in my car, and Frank's smell just seems to pour all over me. I can smell him while he's fuckin' me in the john, then I smell death creepin' out of his mouth. Sometimes I think his smell is seepin' out of my pores, like he's a permanent part of me. Like Rock.

Marilyn

Marilyn (as in Monroe), in her sixties now, is still a glamour puss but very wise.

I'll never forget the message: "Roy wants to talk to Norma Jean."

I was in New York, living with Arthur. It was 1960 when every man in America who didn't want to fuck Marilyn Monroe wanted to fuck Rock Hudson. And every woman in America who didn't want to fuck Rock Hudson wanted to fuck Marilyn Monroe.

I'd just finished making *Let's Make Love* with Yves Montand in a role that Roy had turned down. At first, I thought maybe that's why he was calling. When they were talking about Rock playing opposite me, I told Arthur, "Well, at least you won't have to worry about me fucking my leading man." As it turns out, I did have an affair with Yves. Simone Signoret got the Oscar that year; I got her husband. And, believe me, her husband was just as big as the Oscar.

The Oscar nominations were why Roy called me. Ostensibly. To be honest, I wasn't paying a lot of attention to the Academy Awards at that point in my life; I was more concerned with being an actress. I was studying with Lee Strasberg at the Actors Studio; I was taking acting very seriously.

Roy called to say he was sorry I hadn't been nominated for *Some Like It Hot*. "Can you believe Doris is nominated?" he asked. Well, of course I could believe it. Doris Day was what they liked: as bland as vanilla and just as sickening sweet. What Roy really couldn't believe is that Doris was nominated for *Pillow Talk* and he wasn't. What did he want me to say? I felt certain he didn't want to hear the truth.

Roy and I were sex symbols; nobody really took us seriously. And he was gay. The only thing in Hollywood worse than being a woman is being gay. Everyone knew about him—except those horny housewives in Ohio who wanted to hump him. I suppose he should have won and Oscar for that. He certainly knew how to fake it—which is the reason why they reward you in Hollywood.

I knew how to fake it, too. Marilyn was a fake. That walk, that voice (which I still can't get rid of). I put on Marilyn Monroe like a pair of earrings; Roy put on Rock Hudson like a jockstrap.

He was in a lot of pain when he called. I could hear ice tinkling from his drink. I'd begun drinking champagne—no loud ice. Several times during our conversation, he'd order someone to get him a cigarette, get him a "drank."

He was really obsessed about the Academy Awards— that's all he would talk about even though I'd try to steer the conversation in another direction. I knew he wanted to tell me something but he couldn't; he just couldn't reveal himself; he couldn't be honest. So I did most of the talking.

I told him about all the things I thought we had in common: We were about the same age; we both had these horrific childhoods; we became actors in order to escape; we sought approval; we gave up our real names; we were manufactured by the studio system; we became stars; we were considered pieces of meat; we looked for father figures; we got fucked in order to feel whole; we drank; we lost ourselves.

But talking on the phone that night, there were dramatic differences: we were separated by more than the miles from Hollywood to New York and linked only circumstantially by not being nominated for an Oscar (unlike Doris Day and Simone Signoret). I spent thousands of hours on the couch; I had a phone book filled with the names of good shrinks. Rock refused to seek help. He was a victim; I tried—God knows I tried—to change. I knew I was more than Marilyn

Monroe; he thought he was only Rock Hudson. I was rocking the Hollywood boat; he was passive.

During that phone call, it occurred to me that—unless he changed—he would go to his grave a pathetic, unhappy man. Didn't matter what he died from. I couldn't tell him that but I was able to say how much I wanted to be an artist, how I was no longer able to separate my personal life from my professional life.

You have to work at both, I said. I wanted to be happy but trying to be happy was almost as difficult as trying to be a good actress.

I wanted to be a true actress. I had been studying with Lee for more than five years. And it helped. I'm certainly not suggesting I wasn't crazy. In fact, when an artist tries to be true, you sometimes feel you're on the verge of some kind of craziness.

I always had this secret feeling I was really a fake, a phony. Roy must have felt that, too. Lee taught me to deal with myself. "You're a human being," he'd say, over and over again. I always thought I had to be more, to put on. "No, you're a human being and you start with yourself." Myself, not Marilyn Monroe; I had to take off Marilyn Monroe.

I thought about being in plays when I was a little girl. Because I was so tall, I'd play the male roles; once I played a king. My acting was true then because I hadn't learned how to hide.

Roy listened. We were about to hang up. He was pretty drunk by this time.

"Norma Jean," he said. "Can I tell you a secret?" There was a long, long pause. Then, very, very softly, he whispered: "There's a little girl in me that I just trample to death."

I began to cry. I knew that little girl; she's the same little girl in me, the same little girl in all of us.

"Roy, honey," I told him, "that little girl is the key to your being a good actor, an artist. That little girl is the key to your being happy. That little girl is the truest part of yourself.

"Without her, you're only able to be Rock Hudson, merely a fraction of who you are. Let her out. Your life depends on it." He hung up. Or maybe someone hung up for him. I never spoke to him again. Until recently, of course.

Reggie

Reggie is an over-the-top old Hollywood queen in his sixties.

I'll never forget the first night I met him. Henrietta threw one of her pisselegant dinner soirees to introduce her latest discovery: Roy Fitzgerald from Winnetka, Illinois. Henry Wilson, also known as Doctor Frankenstein, turned him into Rock Hudson from Hollywood, California. But that night he was straight off a milk truck from the midwest. Well, no, he wasn't straight anything. She was as gay as the rest of us. But considerably prettier. And big. She was a big girl. And a tad—dare I say?—nellie. In fact, most of the party guests were there for a purpose: to see if we could make a man out of this big fruit. Henrietta, sipping her champagne (always with a single floating strawberry) pulled me aside and said, "Reggie, darling, can you do something about his voice?"

I had met Henrietta Wilson a year prior—1946, to be exact—when I arrived in Hollywood to become an actress. From Ohio, where I grew up and graduated from college. Speech and Drama major. Gorgeous mother, rich but ugly father. I inherited her temperament and his looks. That did not make me a candidate for stardom—not in Miss Wilson's eyes. She was no beauty, either, let me tell you; she had the grace of a poodle but the face of a bulldog. The only reason Henrietta had any interest in me was my speech training; I was employed by Miss Wilson to transform some of these lispy, wispy sissies into men suitable for the silver screen.

Rock became one of my many challenges. He was 22 at the time (so was I but I looked 42). He was very green; I was very lavender. We met several times a week and I coaxed him into a lower register; honey, she was practically a soprano.

Definitely not the butchest thing in two pumps. I also worked on his walk, trying to keep those hips from swinging out of joint. Butch School, I called it. She was a good student—eager, ambitious, and, most importantly, malleable. Years later, he would tell the press that his voice lowered after a severe case of laryngitis. By that time, she didn't know what was true and what wasn't. Believe me, I changed her voice; not laryngitis.

By the time Henrietta got him his first job—a bit part in *Fighter Squadron*—he sounded considerably more masculine. Thanks to me. And that face on screen! Believe me, it looked better than it did in person: the sign of a true movie goddess. Of course, there were the others: Tab and Troy and Tad and Trey and all those "T" names. They failed Butch School. Miss Wilson could change their names but she couldn't always change their way of life. Of course, everyone knew Rock was a cocksucker, but he could pass when the cameras started rolling—that's what mattered.

However, as his star ascended, the public wanted to know why she wasn't married. *Confidential* magazine was going to tell them, in vivid detail, but Miss Wilson interceded and kept the true story from being printed. How? By giving them some dirt on one of her less famous clients. Henrietta was an evil bitch, let me tell you.

When Rock did *Giant* in 1955, he appeared on the cover of *Life* magazine as "Hollywood's Most Eligible Bachelor." A month later, Henrietta orchestrated his marriage to Phil Gates—I mean, Phyllis Gates—to hush the rumors. A couple of years later, Phil divorced him, citing "extreme mental cruelty."

Speaking of extreme mental cruelty, I continued working for Henrietta throughout the sixties—even after Miss Hudson gave him the axe. Everyone was always drunk: Rock, Henry, me. Henry drank because Rock dumped him. I drank because I was too ugly and too nellie to get laid. Rock Hudson drank because she was Rock Hudson.

I couldn't work; thank God I didn't need to make much money; my parents had both died and left me a fortune. I barely survived my fortieth birthday, coming to the conclusion there was no place for me in the gay world. Gay? My dear. Nothing gay about it in my book. Judy died and everyone started coming out of the closet in droves. That's when someone started that rumor about Rock and Miss Jim Nabors.

Honey, I decided to go straight back to Ohio and go straight. As in hetero. Electric shock treatments and God, not necessarily in that order. They'd wire me to a machine and show slide projections of naked body parts. Big female breasts: no shock. Big hard peepee: big shock. I got married. Really. To a woman. I think. I suppose she knew I was gay; wouldn't you? We went to church—a lot. We also went on a serious drunk—for the next fifteen years. I discovered hustlers—yes, there are hustlers in Ohio—with hair the color of corn and skin as soft as silk.

I don't even remember hearing about Henrietta dying (he was at the Motion Picture Home, destitute and probably as drunk as I was). But when Rock died, I came to. AIDS. There hadn't been much said about AIDS in Ohio until Rock made the headlines; one newspaper article referred to him as "the sodomite." I thought back to that dinner party when I first met him; whoever thought his life would end like it did? Talk about out of the closet. Hon-ey. All those butch lessons for nothing.

I got a divorce. Tried to stop drinking long enough to get back to California. I didn't know why but I was drawn there, the way I had been drawn there forty years prior. I got a small apartment near Paramount, for old time's sake, I guess. And guess what? I immediately got involved in a theatre company. A gay theatre company. Keeps me off the sauce. I'm in an original play, my dear, playing one of those decrepit old auntie types. Type casting, wouldn't you say? It's a big hit. These young kids think I'm a hoot. I regale them with stories from the old days.

When I caught this monstrous cold that wouldn't go away, one of the boys in the show insisted on taking care of me; they've developed these skills, you know. The cold persisted, week after week. "Well, I'm no spring chicken," I told him. I wasn't used to these California warm days and cool nights. He insisted I go to a doctor. Insisted. And the doctor insisted on giving me That Test.

An old girl like me. I could count the number of times I had sex in the past ten years. "Well, it must have been one of those times," the doctor said when he told me I had pneumacystis.

That was about three months ago. Now I've got a few lesions on my leg. Thank God I don't show off my gams in the play; Betty Grable I'm not. More like Betty Ford, honey.

This kid who takes care of me—Jim is his name—he's got it, too. Takes me to these support meetings. I have a hard time—especially when we pass a hand mirror around the circle. Each one of us has to look in the mirror and say, "I love you just the way you are." Ma-ry. Can you imagine? This tired, old dinosaur loving herself? I try, honey, I try my best. I just inhale, take a deep breath and let the words come stumbling out: "I love you just the way you are." Who knows? One day I just might fall for my own publicity.

Michael

Michael is an openly gay/openly HIV-positive actor in his forties.

As Rock Hudson lie dying, *People* magazine interviewed me: The Only Openly Gay Actor in Hollywood. The article, "Fear and AIDS in Hollywood," quoted me: "I have this fantasy," I said. "Tomorrow they discover a cure for AIDS, and Hudson recovers. I wonder, would he be ostracized from the business? Would he be relegated to playing screaming queens? Or would he simply be allowed to continue his career as an openly gay actor? Would he simply be respected?"

Flashback, the Monday after Easter, 1983. Dear Diary: He was stretched out in a prone position, sweating in the sauna with a towel barely covering the head of his movie star dick. As it swelled and swelled, the towel fell away, revealing Rock's cock. Rock hard.

"Did you have a nice Easter?" he asked, making the obligatory towel talk. We're at Brooks Baths, a reputedly legit bathhouse on Beverly Boulevard, a hop across the street from CBS. Rock Hudson hung out there. Literally.

"I act too much," he said, groaning and stretching his massive body, pretending to cover himself with his towel. He stared at my dick, as hard as Rock's. I was pretending to read a copy of *People* magazine.

"You look familiar," he said. "So do you," I said. We stood, simultaneously.

"Too hot," he said. "Me too," I said.

He sauntered out of the sauna. I followed. He made his way to the john at the end of the corridor, glancing over his shoulder. I followed. He went into a tiny cubicle. I followed.

He closed the door. This was a familiar dance; we both knew it. Honey, talk about being between a Rock and a hard place. I locked the door and he unlocked my throat with his tongue.

Kissing him, I could taste remains of Doris Day's lipstick. I could smell remnants of Liz Taylor's perfume. But I delved into places which were off limits for screen lovers. Did Julie Andrews tickle his nipples? Did Angie Dickinson tackle him from behind? I bet Claudia Cardinale didn't lick his oversized balls; I bet Gina Lollabrigida didn't explore the inside of his asshole with her fingertips. He did not exchange bodily fluids with Linda Evans. This was the real ticket, honey, not Hollywood pillow talk.

Flashback, 1989. Dear Diary: I tested positive. I wonder who it could have been?

It could have been John, my best friend from high school; it could have been Flint, that guy in Griffith Park who looked like Jesus; it could have been Dan/Dan, the Married Man; the one at the baths who called himself "Satan"; the one at the baths who called me "honey"; the one I really did love: Victor. It could have been Rock.

It could have been that teacher, that poet, that mechanic, lawyer, mailman, waiter, construction worker, art director.

Could it have been that Italian with red hair? That singer with all the gold records? That black dude with the small cock? That Hispanic hunk with the pockmarks? That activist with all the tattoos?

It could have been that one I picked up at the bank. That one I picked up at the Seven-Eleven. The Music Center. The Spike. The post office. It could have been Rock.

I remember all of them. If not their names, I remember the shape of their shoulders; I remember the taste of their ears; I remember the firmness of their stomachs; I remember the length of their hair; I remember the craziness of their eyes; I remember the wetness of their assholes; I remember the color of their moustaches; I remember the weight of their balls; I remember the sharpness of their teeth; I remember the pitch of their laughs; I remember the moisture of their underarms; I remember the muscles of their legs; I remember the veins of their arms; I remember the rock hardness of their nipples; I remember the softness of their fingertips; I remember the fatness of their cocks; I remember the thickness of their tongues.

Might have been Ricky. Might have been Franc. Might have been Tom. Might have been Ernest. Might have been Richard. It might have been Rock.

Whether or not it was Rock doesn't really matter, none of them died in vain: not Joe, David, Jeffrey, Brett, Paul, Don, Robert, Myron, Vaughn, Victor, Sylvester, John, Philip. Not even Rock.

Cissy

Cissy Stuff is an imprisoned African American transvestite, thirties.

What that sorry skinhead, neo-Nazi didn't realize was that Miss Cissy Stuff was carrying—along with my mascara and my poppers—a switchblade in her pearl-white sequined evening bag. After he smashed my head open with a baseball bat—darlin', there was blood splattered from the tip top of my M.M. blonde wig to the toes of my J.C. come-fuck-me pumps—I had nothing to do but defend myself. This over-sized prick didn't realize that I've lived a life of self-defense. You look up self-defense in the dictionary and you'll find a picture of Miss Cissy Stuff. In color. To keep from bein' another transvestite statistic, I stabbed this hulking punk in his over-inflated chest. His titties were almost as big as mine (and I've had some serious surgery, darlin') but his balls were nowhere near as big (no way would I cut that equipment off, darlin'). How many times did I stab him? Several. Newspaper reports vary; so do the coroner's. Even if I knew, I'm not sure I'd tell you; it's like revealin' my age. How many times I stabbed him ain't nobody's business—suffice it to say that I killed him before he killed me. That's all anyone needs to know. I had just walked offstage, havin' completed the talent competition. It was the night of the Crystal Ball at this downtown dive and I was competin' for the Supreme Goddess title (which I'd won twice in the past—papers got that wrong, too). I had done Aretha—R-E-S-P-E-C-T, find out what it means to me, sock it to me, sock it to me, sock it to me, sock it to me—and the audience peed. When I walked, triumphantly, into the dressing room (which was

actually the kitchen), all hell had broken lose. About ten skin-
heads, some of them covered with sheets, stormed the place,
beatin' the asses of these defenseless black queens. Only one
of those other divas had that balls to fight back. Miss
Butterfly deQueen was pummelin' one of them putrefied
punks with her Vidal Sassoon hair dryer. I took one look at
my blood-soaked gown (white marabou feathers, darlin', a
small fortune) and grabbed my switchblade. That's when a
couple of the other girls joined me, with kitchen knives.
Except for the one I offed, the pansy-ass motherfuckers ran—
not before firin' a gun and woundin' my worst girlfriend,
Janet Mahalia Jackson. The rest is, as they say, a matter of
record. My public defender was a white heterosexual male.
You know what the opposite of a white heterosexual male is?
I am: a gay black drag queen. I was given the death sentence.
In more ways than one, darlin'. I've been in here five years.
The tuberculosis is brand new; T.B. or not to be: that is
definitely the fucking question. The lesions? A coupla years.
The eye shadow-to-match is brand new. AIDS was added
onto my sentence after I checked in here; so now I'm not sure
if I'll die strapped in the electric chair or strapped to a hospital bed. Either shouting "I want to live" like Susie Hayward
or coughing up blood like Missy Garbo. I was tested, as a
matter of routine, when I arrived for my stay here at the
Holiday Inn for Wayward Girls. Actually, they put me in a
men's prison—odd punishment for a major nellie cocksucker,
wouldn't you say? I tested negative, by the way. Twice. I
wasn't here five minutes before I met Vic. A guard. My
guardian angel. Or my angel of death, dependin' on how you
look at it. A big, burly motherfucker, 250 pounds of hard
flesh, as white as an unopened virgin sheet. I could tell he
liked me upon sight—you just know, y'know. Wife at
home—don't matter, darlin'. He had an immediate hankerin'
for my black ass, if you know what I mean. He also took a
likin' to my black dick. But I'm gettin' a-head of myself, so to
speak. First night I was here he kidnapped me from my cell

and took me to this secret place with a king-size bed and sexy music floatin' outta fancy speakers. Other guards knew his trip; believe me, they had their own trips goin' on. He liked Marvin Gaye music. Funny 'cause it reminded me of Johnny, one of my first loves, who also liked to fuck to the sounds of Miss Gaye. I did the fucking. Johnny liked takin' it up the ass. He called it "sissy stuff." That's how I got my name; seems everything I liked to do was called sissy stuff so I figured that's what I'd call myself: Miss Cissy Stuff. Fucking white butch boys definitely fell under—and I do mean under—the category of sissy stuff. A black nellie drag queen—well, drag princess in those days; a black nellie princess gettin' fucked was redundant. I, like most women, am a top. 'Course big butch Vic had to prove his manhood by fuckin' me first; only then could he lift those big, strong legs in the air and let me drive it into his muscle butt. While Marvin sang, "Mercy, mercy me, things ain't what they used to be . . ." So this became a ritual—at least twice a week, Vic and I had a hot slam session. And the rest of the time, he protected me—or saw to it I was protected—from the rest of the population. What he didn't protect me from was his liquids laced with poison. Darlin', askin' someone to wear a rubber when you're on Death Row is an oxymoron. Vic and I fucked each other without a Trojan in sight. About a year ago, Vic's real wife had a baby, born real sick. Died mysteriously in a matter of months. I didn't put it together until Vic started gettin' sick: high fevers, diarrhea, losin' weight. V-I-C had H-I-V. So when I saw the first blast of purple on my foot—size eleven, same as Jackie—I wasn't surprised. We kept fucking as Vic dwindled from 250 pounds to 125. The incredible shrinking man. AIDS didn't make us any less horny, honey, just a little less photogenic. The night Vic's real wife died—about six months after he lost his baby boy—nobody could believe it but he insisted on showin' up for work. Eventually we wound up in bed where I fucked him raw. "Mercy, mercy me." I remember, after it was over, he kissed every inch of my diseased body, including those fuchsia polka dots. It was like he was celebratin' or somethin'. That was the last time I saw my guardian angel. Vic went home that morning and shot himself in the mouth. The mouth that had kissed me all over, over and over, all over. Now I'm in isolation, coughing up blood. Not pretty. Contagious. Nothin' new for me, darlin'. People have always treated Miss Cissy Stuff like she's contagious. But now—vether I vant to or not—like La Garbo, I am alone.

Bud

Bud is a Vietnam vet, forties.

I was no virgin when it came to death. Or headlines. My journey to Death Row was littered with a batch of front page headline deaths. Before I was one fuckin' year old, a fireman rescued me from a burning building that killed my drunken mommy and daddy. That big nigger got his face on the front page of the paper for rescuin' a helpless, boohooin' baby. Yesterday, 41 years and about 41 foster parents later, Mother Theresa made the front page, trying to rescue me by convincin' the Governor to pardon my imminent execution. My lawyers are tryin' to prove I'm the victim of FAS: Fetal Alcohol Syndrome, also known as Fucked At Start. To think all the time I been spending planning my last meal might be in vain. I'm gonna order chocolate-covered everything, by the way. In honor of my predilections; in my case, that's pre-de-lick-tions. I'd be a great spokesman for Hershey's. "What will satisfy my craving hunger before my stroll to the electric chair? Hershey's, that's what." The first time I ever tasted chocolate was in Vietnam. Willy. That nigger died in my fuckin' arms. Shot in the chest, right through his juicy black heart. The blood didn't seem real, though; it was Technicolor, movie blood, gushing from his massive chest. He was a goner, man. Where was Oliver Stone? Everything was in slow fucking motion. Even the gushing blood spurted slowly. Slowly, very slowly, my dick began to grow. Harden. Burstin' outta my fatigues. Now let's get something straight: except for that coal-black fire fighter who saved my lily-white ass, I hated niggers. And I was not a homosexual. I'd never in my life had a homosexual experience. I never knew a living homosexual. I couldn't even spell homosexual. But for whatever reason, for whatever unfuckingexplainable reason, I had a boner. And I had this overfuckingpowering desire to kiss Willy. Kiss that big dead nigger on his big dead nigger lips. He was my bud, my man, by bro. It was almost like I was watchin' myself in a fuckin' movie. A fag porno movie. I kissed the motherfucker—on the mouth. His mouth opened. Was he alive? Shit, no. But his mouth invited me in. His tongue moved. I licked his tongue with my tongue. Tasted like licorice—not black but cherry. Delicious. I sucked his tongue. Then I watched myself unbutton his fatigues and next thing I knew I was chewing on his dick. Was it getting hard? Shit, no. But it tasted good—like a juicy fuckin' piece of meat. Dead meat. I was jackin' myself off with my right hand, cryin' at the same time, and sliding my left hand across Willy's chest, trying to feel his heart beat. Pushin' on his heart. Trying to jump start his heart. I wanted his heart. To eat. To keep. I wanted to eat his heart. Keep his heart. For a souvenir. To remember him by. That's all I remember. Willy was not the first person to leave me. Or the last. I went to Vietnam when I was seventeen. Willy was my only friend. My buddy. "Bud," he called me. The first nigger I'd ever talked to in my entire life. The first person I ever talked to in my life. He was a tough motherfucker. Strong as they come. We were meant for each other— peers, not queers. No equals in the toughness test. No one dared fuck with me or Willy. And as a team, we were infuckingdestructible. There wasn't a queer bone in either of our bodies. As far I was concerned, that slow motion flick never happened. According to the psychiatrists, I buried that experience when they buried Willy. After Vietnam, I got married. But did not live happily ever after. She divorced me because I was fucked up, drugged up, out of my mind, down and out, insane and in pain. Got married a second time. Struck out again; this one said I had a violent streak. What I had, it turned out, was a violet streak. I discovered my dark passion—my dark purple passion—in a neighborhood park where I'd been scorin' drugs for years. I'd never paid any attention to the dark meat market, the packs of pubescent punks, ebony skin glistening against the pitch black night. One of 'em sold me some heavy speed and offered a discount if I wanted him, too. The opposite of a white sale. At first I didn't know what he meant until I realized the shape of his nose reminded me of Willy's nose and the sweat on his naked chest smelled like Willy's sweat. I wondered if his tongue would taste like Willy's; if his heart would thump like Willy's. My dick was hard. I don't remember cutting out his tongue; I don't remember slicing open his chest; I don't remember hacking off his cock. I don't remember the blood, the cum, the shit, the piss. All I remember is sleeping with him; him in my arms, asleep. Knowing he would not leave me. Left is not the opposite of right. Left is what everyone in my fuckin' life has done to me: they left. The opposite of right is wrong. Wrong to leave me. So I kept him, asleep in that bed, for days—until people in the building began to ask me about the smell. Wouldn't that be a motherfucker of a commercial? "You probably don't believe I've had a dead body in my bed for days since you can't smell a thing except pine trees, thanks to my disinfectant spray." Unfortunately, no amount of Lysol would eliminate the sweet stench. I had to say goodbye, but he didn't leave me. I was in control for the first time in my life. When I buried him—in the backyard next to a bad-luck black cat I'd accidentally run over one night when I was drunk—I thought of Willy's burial. I could hear "Taps" playin' in the distance. There were others I buried there— some leaner, some juicier, some with fatter dicks, some with thicker nipples, some were tougher, some were more tender. All reminded me of Willy. I was their Bud. I always heard "Taps" playin' in the distance. I buried them all, one next to the other, storing delicious mementos—an ear, a shoulder blade, a particularly overripe thigh—in one of those huge freezers I bought at Circuit City. *(Commercial)* "A freezer roomy enough to hold choice body parts of several of your closest friends." It became my hope chest. Hope I never got caught. But I did. The newspapers say I wanted to—get caught, that is—buryin' my chocolate-covered soldiers right in my own backyard. Maybe so. I made the cover of *People* magazine. Rap groups have written songs about me. The President mentioned me in one of his televised addresses. Geraldo has become a personal friend of mine. I'm gonna invite him to the execution. It's only five days away. Thank God I haven't lost my sense of humor. We get to choose our spiritual adviser, y'know. I think I made a juicy choice: Denzel Washington.

Joey

Joey is a Hispanic pretty boy in his twenties.

"Fuck my Jew fag pussy until I bleed," he said, after shooting himself up the ass with crystal meth. The only time he admitted he was a Jew—or a fag, or a pussy—was in bed. Drugged-up. I met Len ("Whatever you do, don't call me Lenny; it sounds too Jewish") on Sunset, near Laurel Canyon. He had just been to a screening at the Director's Guild. I'd just had a drink, across the street, at Numbers. He practically ran over me with his fire-engine red Jag. I wasn't hustling; shit, I wasn't even hitchhiking. I was walking to my car when he stopped me. The first thing I noticed, on the passenger seat, were the trade papers: *Variety* and the *Hollywood Reporter*. "You need a lift?" he said, ignoring the car keys in my hand. That moment. If I could go back to that second of seduction, knowing what I do now. "Yeah," I said, stuffing the keys into the pocket of my skintight Calvins. He began driving to his house on Coldwater Canyon. If it was a movie, the credits would be rolling. My fate was predetermined in those few fucking minutes. I recognized his name—Len Conners—even though his face, with its too-small nose, didn't register. He wasn't as handsome as he was groomed: glowing skin (even though there were pockmarks); glaringly manicured nails; great hair (which I'd later discover was transplanted, like doll hair); groovy black Armani suit and gorgeous tie, splattered with bright red splotches. He drove too fast and spoke too loud on the red car phone, ordering a meal for us (using words I can't pronounce). His tone was superior and condescending. "And plenty of Dom Perignon," he barked, slamming down the phone and gunning the gas pedal.

Switching demeanor—and gears—he whispered, "Are you an actor? If you aren't you should be." I told him I'd played Henry Higgins in a high school play. "George Cukor directed the movie!" he announced, loud again, like he was answering the bonus question on Jeopardy. I pointed out that I was in *Pygmalion*, not *My Fair Lady*. "Pig-what?" he said, never having heard of it. Without even waiting for an answer, he seized the moment. "Cukor won the Oscar for *My Fair Lady*. 1964. Audrey lost to Julie for Mary Fucking Poppins. More that 20 years before I won my Oscar." That's right, I remembered, he'd produced one of those feel-good movies back when I was still in high school. There are several things I remember about that first night: the oversized bottle of poppers, sitting next to his Oscar, on an elaborate table next to his bed; red satin sheets and pillowcases; a huge collection of ties, all of them streaked with shades of red (like presidential candidate ties, only infinitely more glamorous). The first time he kissed me, he bit my lip until it bled. "I like the taste of blood," he said, "I like the smell of red." Before the night was over, we'd snorted that bottle of poppers, drunk several bottles of "Dom" (as he called it); I'd tied him up with his "power ties" (as he called them); and we'd soiled the red satin sheets and pillowcases with a flood of body fluids. I remember one more thing: He promised me he was HIV negative. So was I. The next day he sent me five dozen red roses, and a card which had the keys to his house taped to it. "My house is your house," the card read. I moved in about a week later. I'm not sure why; I felt hypnotized or something weird. I was simultaneously repulsed by him and attracted to him. He had this power. As the weeks turned into months, I began to despise him and everything he stood for. He was mean. The sex got kinkier. Schizophrenic. When he fucked me (without a rubber), he'd call me a faggot spic, a puto, a Mexican pussy. Then he'd order me to fuck him. Once he had me stick the Oscar up his butt. "Make my Jew fag pussy red," he'd say. This sex was not lovemaking; it was hate mongering. He took control of my life, trying to make me a star. Changed my name from Jose to Joey; from Aguilar to Glar ("rhymes with star," he'd say). "You can pass," he'd repeat, like a campaign slogan. "You can pass." He got me some interviews with some of his casting director friends ("faggot list-makers," he'd say behind their backs). "Tell them about your girlfriend; keep your legs uncrossed; lower your voice; don't smile too much," he instructed. I had become Eliza Doolittle. He insisted I start playing sports—specifically, baseball. To butch me up. He bought me all this baseball equipment: the right shoes, the right glove, the right bat. "You can pass—especially if you butch it up." Every Sunday, he'd throw these out-landish parties for Hollywood's closeted queers. And he'd hire hookers for them—"extras," he'd call them. Some were hired as bartenders; others were professional sunbathers; a couple could even play tennis. What the extras all had in common was the ability to fuck anything that moved. They were most-ly white blondes with overinflated tits and painted-on tan lines. Naked, they'd sit poised on the edge of the pool, ready to dive in, like trained dolphins (but not nearly as smart). I met them all at these dreary parties: Sandy and Barry, Chamberlain and Maharis. I also met Cooper Ventura, one of the last actors who'd been named by Henry Wilson (Cooper after Gary, Ventura after the freeway). Cooper was pushing 50 and had just come out on *Entertainment Tonight*, shocking all those middle-American fans who had watched him play a hot-to-trot hetero for years on a daytime soap. I admired Cooper for coming out; Len hated him for it. "That overripe faggot has-been," he'd snarl. "This could hurt the rest of us." When Cooper suddenly stopped attending the Sunday sissy soirees, I realized he'd been blacklisted by Len. I found his number in the Rolodex—after Jack Valenti and before Gore Vidal—and called him. We began seeing each other. Cooper was everything Len wasn't: gentle, loving, considerate. Len thought he owned me and would kill me if he found out about Cooper. I knew I had to get out. But how? I was in too deep. It got pretty bad. Len became suspicious when I couldn't force myself to have sex with him anymore. I felt like I was being followed. I was paranoid. I couldn't sleep. One night, he went to a screening with Lucie Arnaz (never with me in public, of course) and I tried desperately to fall asleep. I decided to ransack his medicine cabinet in search of sleeping pills. There, in the midst of eye cremes and astringents and lip gloss and rubbers and a fucking eyelash curler, behind the Valium and the nembutal, there was a small white bottle, labeled "Retrovir," filled with little blue-and-white capsules. AZT. He had been murdering me all along. For months. How many times had he fucked me? Infected me? Standing in the bathroom, at the medicine cabinet, I could hear him stumbling around in the bedroom. He was home early, not a good sign. "You sleazy slutty spic," he slurred, sounding slightly smashed. He was clutching that goddam Oscar. "I'm going to kill you, you whore." "You already have," I said. He didn't hear me; he just started screaming. Hysterically. Like a woman. About Cooper. "You two sissy faggots deserve each other," he shrieked. Then he clipped my head with the Oscar. Twice, I remember. The details blur. I was bleeding. He was suddenly bleeding. Next thing I knew I had that baseball bat in my hand, both hands, swinging it across his back, his legs, his head. Smashing the shit out of him. I could hear bones crunching. I remember him pulling his pants down as I disassembled his plastic nose. I remember him pulling on his dick. The pathetic asshole's fucking dick was hard. (The police report failed to mention that; so did *Hard Copy* and *Inside Edition.* They called it murder; I call it a suicide pact.) Blood was squirting, spurting everywhere—in my eyes, in my mouth, maybe even up my ass. It smelled good. It smelled red. Like power.

Chuck

Chuck is an African American hunk, thirty something.

Admit it: You think one of two things when you see a black man. You either think I'm going to fuck you or kill you. Or both. When you hear the two words "black man," you think the two words "big dick." A black dick is universally revered or feared; to be feared or commandeered. Whether you consider me subhuman or superhuman; whether you suck dick or eat pussy; whether you are a heartbeat darker than me or a mile lighter; whether you take it up your ass, in your cunt, or down your throat; whether you are 16 or 65; whether you graduated with honors or can't spell "honors"; whether you live uptown or down. There's one thing you have in common: You are besieged with intrigue about my black dick. You might want to chop it off; you might want to marry it. Either way, it has power over you. My name is Chuck, rhymes with suck, fuck, buck, bad luck. "That thing could kill me," he said, caressing my throbbing cock. He was speaking metaphorically, complimenting me on the longness, the wideness, the thickness of my dick, as many before him had. But this time it was different. My pride-and-joy, my prize, my pet, my calling card could kill him. My jizz, my juice, my jackoff jam was as poisonous as a rattlesnake. Hissss. My dick had always been an effective tool but now it was a sword, an arrow, a knife, a machete. A loaded machine gun, aching to rat-a-tat-tat its vicious venom into mouths, down throats and up buttholes. 'Til death do us part, baby. D.O.D., D.O.A. Dick of Death, Dead on Arrival. "Yeah, that thing could kill you," I moaned, getting it slippery with my own infected spit. "Are you gonna put on a condom?" the pussy whined, like a carefully taught schoolboy, not even comfortable enough to say "rubber." "Yeah, sure," I said, remembering how I'd deliberately perforated the end of the rubber I was carrying in my pocket. My first victim. A beauty. A whore. A pretty boy slut. A tease. The only reason he paid attention to me was my dick. He'd pay for that. The hard way, baby. I was sick of being everybody's dick—men, women, boys and girls. Whores and faggots, pussies and pricks. Lions and tigers and bears. Mommy. When your first blow job—before my first Holy Communion—is from your mother, you realize you got somethin' special between your legs. When she wasn't on her knees in front of me, she was at church—on her knees. I went to a mostly white Catholic school and since I never heard any of the other boys talkin' about their mothers givin' 'em head, I figured this was something only niggers did. A coupla years later, this crazy ass drunken uncle began blowin' me on a regular basis. We were a very close family; closer than the fuckin' Cosbys. By the time I got into junior high, I can remember white pussyboys in the shower starin' at my peter. Salivatin' at the thought of it. Fuck those faggots. If they looked too hard, or got too hard lookin', I'd get harder, and beat the shit out of them. I was destined to be a ladies' man—even fucked my English teacher to prove it. "Rape me," she kept saying, over and over—even though the white bitch had asked me to come to her house to do some handiwork. Workin' with my hands was only part of the job; what I did was some dick work. "Rape me," she said. I got a fuckin' A in English; I guess she figured my dick knew the difference between a verb and a noun because I sure the fuck didn't. The only thing she taught me was that my dick is a noun and a verb. I fucked a lot of pussy before I finished high school, before I left home. And the more I fucked, the angrier I got: at broads, at faggots, at Mommy, at Uncle Twinkletoes, at myself. By this time, my cocksucking mother spent more time at home on her knees than at church. She had "boyfriends", some of 'em at least 60 fuckin' years old, but she called them boyfriends. They came and they went, so to speak, like my father, obviously. I went when I couldn't take it anymore. I was not destined to be another Michael Jackson or another Michael Jordan, so I began sellin' it in the seventies. To men. Guys would pay to photograph it, sit on it, lick it, put whipped cream on it, drink piss out of it, step on it, bite it, put out cigarettes on it, stick it up their ass, push it down their throat, cover it with Crisco, eat shit off it, pour hot candle wax on it, slurp chocolate off it, slap their face with it, gag on it, clean their own blood off of it. I musta made a hundred thousand dollars off my big black dick. And became one of those fags, like I used to beat up, in the process. By the time I turned 30, I understood what it was like to get on your knees and pray to not get on your knees. Before you could say "cocksucker," I was just another pathetic homo in pursuit of legendary dicks to penetrate every part of me—except my heart. Feelings were never part of the exchange. I might have become a fag but I wasn't a romantic. Love was not in my vocabulary. "Rape me" was. Sometime in the eighties—when I was too old to sell it and too young to buy it—I met my Terminator. Someone shot me up with their murderous sperm, their killer cum, their loaded load. Did my killer give me a clue? Did he kiss me goodbye and mean it? Did he wish me luck? Did he know? Did he know I was his victim? His prey? His target? I've since lost count of my conquests, my concubines, my companions in death. I will take them with me: the blue-eyed blondes with zero IQ, the swarthy types right out of GQ, the musclemen, the married men, the butches, the femmes, the tops, the bottoms, the S's, the M's. We're in this together, brothers. This is the gay parade to the cemetery and I've elected myself grand fucking marshall, dude.

Carmen

Carmen is a Hispanic woman, sixtyish.

"You brought me into this world, now you can take me out of it." My son, Juan, began shouting these words at me seven weeks before. Before he died. Before his death. "You brought me into this world," he'd shout with the little bit of strength he had left. Near the end, he'd barely whisper, "Now you can take me out of it." His voice—a voice which sang lullabies to his mother and show tunes on Broadway—was an old man's croak. No strength. He had no strength. For seven weeks, the doctor predicted each week would be his last. Everyday, for seven weeks, I prepared myself to say goodbye to my Juan, my mijo. Even though he wanted to, he could not die. Even though he wanted to, he would not die. And even though he wanted to, he "should not die," I told his friends, believing in God's will to take him when he was ready. "Of course I cannot kill you, mijo. What are you saying? Are you out of your mind?" I would yell back at him. We always loved a good fight, both of us. "You are my son, my flesh and blood. I am your mother." "And that is why it is your responsibility," he would say, coughing and gasping for air. There were nights when he was out of his mind. Talking crazy talk. Sex talk. When I arrived to take care of him, he could still walk; he could still see; he could still make sense. He told me he was ill in January. He told me how ill he was in February. He told me it was AIDS in March. That's when I packed a suitcase and placed it by the front door, exactly the same as I had when he was inside me, when I was prepared to give birth to him. Inside me, kicking and squirming, coming alive. Now I was prepared to watch him die. I made him promise he would tell him Mamita when he needed her. He'd never break a promise. He was always a good boy—especially when it came to his Mama. His father and I moved from Cuba to Florida when he was a little boy. His father was rough on Juan because he was a delicate child. He loved me—my clothes, my shoes, my makeup. He liked nothing more than to dress up and dance. When he heard Tchaikovsky on the radio—he couldn't have been more than six or seven—he had to have that particular recording. Behind his father's back, I went out and bought it with my food allowance. It turned out to be the "Dance of the Sugar Plum Fairies." He'd dance to that record like a little changito. Monkey. If his father caught him, he'd smack him hard across the face. He could only dress in my clothes and dance to Tchaikovsky when we were alone together. It was our secret ritual. On nights when his father didn't come home, Juan would sing me to sleep— songs he'd make up as he went along. By the time he was a teenager, I divorced his cruel father. And sent my mijo to dancing school with my alimony money. After high school, he was good enough to go to New York and get a job dancing in the chorus. Over the next twenty years, he was good to his Mama. He'd bring me to New York (I saw him in *A Chorus Line* more than once and *Gatos* three or four times—*Cats*); he'd send me postcards from all over the world; he paid me back for those dancing lessons a hundred times over. He never actually told me he was gay. I think he just knew I knew; mothers do. When he called to tell me it was time for me to come take care of him, he warned me that I wouldn't recognize him. Nothing could have prepared me for the sight of my beautiful boy. Practically bald, sunken eyes, caved in chest, and legs like toothpicks. His legs had been full of muscle, as sturdy as tree trunks, dancing around the world and back. When I arrived, he could barely keep his balance to walk across the room. In a matter of weeks, he was in a wheelchair. Then he completely lost his vision and had to stay in bed. He refused to eat. The doctor had run out of remedies and only prescribed pain medication. "Is there enough to off me?" Johnny asked (he'd changed his name to Johnny when he got into show business). Even though he was blind and helpless, I hid the pills in a bottom drawer of his dresser which was full of silky women's underwear. He had dozens of friends who helped me take care of him around the clock. I was afraid he might convince one of them to give him an overdose. But not me. Thank God he had so many friends. It took two of us to handle him. Because he couldn't see, one person had to be his eyes. Because he couldn't walk, the other had to be his legs. We would lead him to the bathroom, propping him up, guiding him. The walls of his bathroom were lined with photos of him—photos of him in shows, photos of him with big stars, photos of him dancing, laughing, smiling. Photos of him with gorgeous men, looking all kinds of handsome. Sitting on the toilet was an old man, not the incredibly alive boy in the photographs. It became impossible to move him from the bed to the bathroom so we diapered him. My baby hated it. "You brought me into this world, now you can take me out of it," he started chanting. His friends came to help in eight-hour shifts. Rarely was I ever alone with him. I admit I liked it when someone was late or the rare occasion when someone called to say they couldn't make it. It reminded me of being alone with him, when his father was away, when he'd dance to the sugar plum song. I was alone with him one night, sleeping in the bed next to him, when there was an unexpected knock at the door. It was about 2:00 A.M. "I know you're in there, Johnny," this guy on the other side of the door said, in a deep, booming voice. "I saw your car. Let me in, you sexy motherfucker." I opened the door. "I'm Carmen, Juan's mother," I told this big man, dressed in black leather from head to foot, carrying what looked like a doctor's bag. He had a ring through his nose and tattoos decorating the muscles of his huge arms. He apologized. His eyes were dark, wild, magnetic. "Juan is very sick," I told him. "I didn't know," he said. "Can I see him?"

There were tears in his eyes. I put on a fresh pot of coffee. We talked and talked, mostly about Juan/Johnny. His name was Michael; Juan, he said, called him Miguelito. Both names seemed inappropriately soft for this macho man. I learned more about my son than I ever expected I would. "He was a hot fuck," Miguelito said. "The best I ever had. Ever. You gave birth to a wild man." When I told him that Juan wanted me to end his life, Miguelito did not blink. When Juan stirred in the bedroom, making an animal sound, Miguelito again asked if he could see him. I asked him if he would help me change his diaper. Simply and politely, he said, "Your son's shit doesn't bother me, Carmen." In fact, we had to change the sheets in addition to the baby's diaper. Juan was practically in a coma, barely able to grunt and gurgle. Miguelito was incredibly gentle with him. "Easy, stud," he'd say as we lifted him and shifted him on the bed. His massive hands caressingly cleansed what was left of Juan's purple polka-dotted body. He refused to put on rubber gloves. "I want to feel him," he said. By the time we finished, Juan looked as peaceful as I'd seen him in weeks. He almost seemed to be smiling. Miguelito lit some candles which he took from his black leather satchel. He told me how much Juan liked candles; he always brought them when he came over to play. He also brought a tape of Juan's favorite music which he made for him. "He'd be more comfortable in these," Miguelito said, pulling out a pair of women's black, silky panties. "A tribute to you," he said with a wink. "He's ready," Miguelito said. "Ready?" I asked. "You know," he said, putting on a pair of black leather gloves. "Your baby/my baby loved the smell of leather. Let's hope he hasn't lost his sense of smell." He then said we would "help each other deliver our baby." He turned on the special music tape, very softly. Then he put his leather-gloved hand over Juan's nose and placed my hand over his mouth. It didn't take long. When it was over, Miguelito blew out the candles and put them, along with the soiled panties, in his black bag. It wasn't until he turned it off that I realized what music had been playing: The Dance of the Sugar Plum Fairies. After this vision in black floated out of the apartment, I followed the list of instructions I'd made for myself: Call the doctor. "My son died," I told him. "Peacefully, very peacefully."

Neal

Neal is a gay white boy, forties.

Sammy was Ethel to my Lucy. He was this outrageously
funny Jewish boy who lived down the street from me when I
was a kid in Augusta, Georgia; kinda Harvey Fiersteinish—
even then. A Jew in the South is kinda like a heterosexual on
Fire Island. We were best friends, our bond cemented by our
obsession with the *I Love Lucy* show. We would watch an
episode and then go down into my basement and act it out
with an imaginary Ricky and Fred. The summer my family
moved away from Augusta—I must have been 9 or 10—
Sammy's family was going on vacation. To Hollywood! I was
crazed with jealousy which eventually quelled into a pride-by-
association. It wasn't everyone who knew someone taking a
journey to where the real Lucy lived. My parents, two brothers and I moved to St. Louis, and I only heard from Sammy
once or twice—a postcard from the Brown Derby and a letter
telling me, sadly, he never met Lucy. I missed him terribly
and distinctly remember realizing I loved him more—and in
a different way—than I did my brothers. Or even my Mom
and Dad. I felt guilty about that fact so I never told anyone,
not even Sammy. We lost touch with each other. The next
time I ran into Sammy was about twenty years later. In a gay
bar in L.A., only a few miles away from the house in Beverly
Hills where Lucy lived all those years. We became insepara-
ble, resuming our Lucy and Ethel roles, acting out with a
vengence, turning our lives into Lucy episodes. Lucy and
Ethel Go to the Baths. Lucy and Ethel See Barbara in Vegas,
Lucy and Ethel Bump Pussies and Try On Hats. Lucy and
Ethel Take a Mud Bath. Lucy and Ethel Visit Marilyn in

Westwood. Lucy and Ethel Join a 12-Step Program. Lucy and Ethel Visit Anne Frank's House. Lucy and Ethel Test Positive. Lucy and Ethel See Ann-Margret at Radio City. Lucy and Ethel Become Roommates. Lucy and Ethel Go On Disability. Lucy and Ethel Get Sick. Just last night we came up with a script, our final Lucy and Ethel caper. Imagine. Lucy and Ethel didn't die, those two broads are still on prime time. Ricky and Fred are long gone but the girls, in their eighties, are living in a nursing home. They are both pretty emaciated. On some occasions, Ethel needs to be padded since Lucy's contract still insists she remain thinner than Ethel. Lucy's hair is defiantly bright red but occasionally the grey roots show. Ethel is bald from chemotherapy but wears a plucky blonde wig. Ethel is in a wheelchair. Lucy walks with a cane (which proves to be a great prop). Both of them are in the advanced staged of dementia. But they are still up to their same old antics—like trying to get into show business. But the network, knowing they're on the verge of kicking, orders the final episode and wants it to be 1992 humor—a little kinky, like *Northern Exposure*. The last show, titled "Joining the Boys", will depict Lucy and Ethel's final act of zaniness: double suicide. The episode opens with Lucy on the phone to Dr. Jack Kervokian (playing himself, in a special guest appearance). When it becomes clear he can't assist, the girls decide to proceed on their own. As they make the final arrangements—writing their wills, calling Little Lucie and Desi Jr.—we see flashbacks of the twosome in those famous episodes: in the chocolate factory, at the Brown Derby in Hollywood, on the top of the Empire State Building in New York. It's an hour special. As the moment of reckoning comes, the audience thinks they're going to botch it in typical Lucy and Ethel fashion. But we don't. We decide on sleeping pills, which we've been storing up faithfully, and vodka. Ethel/Sammy agrees to go first so I/Lucy will have the final moment: a direct address to the audience. He, Sammy, died a few minutes ago. He agreed to go first. We did it, double suicide, like Lucy and Ethel would have. "Joining the Boys." Everybody dies: Lucy, Ethel, Ricky, Fred, Sammy, me. *(Sings)* "I love Sammy and he loves me, we're happy as we can be . . ."

MIJO

Michael

Michael is an African American gay man in his late thirties.

When I was a little boy, we lived on a street which butted up against a cemetery. To avoid my half-dead family, I would escape there with a pack of bullying school bruisers who delighted in deriding me. "Sissy," they'd venomously hiss. And believe me, the only thing worse than being a white sissy is being a black sissy. We'd hide out among the dead, proving our fearlessness, trying to pronounce names on gravestones, sniffing gladiolus on the fresh graves of the most recently departed and occasionally confiscating lavender or pink ribbons inscribed with the words "My Brother" or "Dear Son" or "Loving Husband" made from metallic gold stick-on letters. On one of our trips to the land of the dead, we heard the whimpering sounds of a suffering animal, buried in a pile of orange and amber leaves. Nearby was the bloodied branch of a tree, remnants of a brutal St. Louis storm the day before. The sturdy stick had obviously struck the animal, wounding it without killing it. I couldn't even see the crying animal—I think it was a squirrel—but I could feel its unremitting pain. What do we do? There was only one moral choice: I must kill it, cease its endless lifelessness, silence its cries. The other boys—champions of gym class, heroes on the basketball court—were rendered uncharacteristically limp, deflated by the animal's helplessness. As they scurried in all directions, I searched for a weapon, finding a large rock, more like a boulder, which would deliver the small beast from its misery. With all my might, I hurled the rock in the direction of my pathetic victim, still hidden under the autumn leaves, over and over again I threw it, until there was no more sound.

Never, in my short life, had I experienced such a stirring silence, such a staggering peace of mind, such a stunning tranquility. At that very moment, the sun appeared, illuminating the ground where I would bury my prey. Using the very branch which had randomly targeted the innocent animal, I dug a makeshift grave. Without ever looking at the small creature, I scooted it into the grave, amidst the sun-drenched golden leaves. For decoration, I stole some blood-red gladiolus and a deep purple ribbon from a nearby grave. I was no longer a powerless sissy. I knew the difference between right and wrong, good and bad, evil and spiritual. As quickly as it appeared, the sun evaporated and it began to sprinkle. In a frenzy of ecstasy, I ripped off my clothes and danced in the pouring rain. The harder it poured, the harder I danced. I must have danced until I passed out from joyfulness. When I woke up, lying naked on the grave of my loved one, it had stopped raining and the sky was pitch black. I threw on my soaking wet clothes and stumbled over the freshly muddied graves until I instinctively found my way home. No one even knew I'd been gone and no one cared about my elegiac epiphany. But I knew I would never be the same.

MYRON

Myron

Myron is an African American gay man, fortyish.

In love? In hate, maybe. I hated myself; I hated queers; I hated niggers. I either wanted to be white or straight or both. A black nellie faggot did not win popularity contests. Straight blacks hated me because I was gay. Gay blacks hated me because I was nellie. Gay whites hated me because I was black and nellie. But there was always some dinge queen in the johns or the bushes or the baths. However, contrary to what you read in *Penthouse* and/or *Honcho*, not all black dudes are hung like black stallions. The ones who thought they was gonna get a big piece a meat got a big disappointment instead. Oh, there were flashes of being okay, glimmers of connections. A few encounters which had meaning: the occasional black man who was comfortable enough to make love, not just have sex, with another black guy; the occasional white man who really seemed not to be another racist size-dinge queen. But mostly there were queers, black and white, who hated themselves as much as I hated myself. We'd engage in this tango of self-hate, acting out our racism, playing with our homophobia. You wanna talk slave and master? Honey, I could go both ways: I'd play Uncle Tom one day and Diana Ross/The Boss the next. But whether I was on top or on my knees, I thought sex would fix it. And for a while—from about 1975 to 1985—it did. In love? You've got to be kidding. The most loving sex I ever had? I think about it a lot. It was at the baths, probably fifteen year ago. And even though I was probably pretty tweeked at the time. I remember it vividly. This black kid, not pretty in that slick way but real pretty to me, and I were making out. Kissing, passionately. In my experience, not many queers kissed. And not many black queers kissed each other. As I said most of them wanted some white meat, period. This boy—I don't remember his name— was a great kisser. Then all of a sudden, in the midst of this romantic kissing interlude, he says to me, "I want you to fist me." Even though I knew. he said "fist," I acted like he said "kiss." "I want you to stick your hand inside my butt," he said, making himself perfectly clear. So I did. It was an incredibly powerful experience—one I never had the guts to write about. It was intimate and it was connected and it was all of the things those fist-fucking queens said it was. And the fact he was a black boy, giving himself to me, was part of it. It was emotional. I'd been used to all sorts of rejection from pretty black boys. So to have my hand—my arm, to be hon-est—inside him was amazing. But after I came, jacking myself off, watching my arm slide in and out of his ass, I felt guilt like I'd never felt before. For days, I would scrub my hands, clean my fingernails. I could smell Crisco on my arm for weeks. I was like Lady Macbeth: "Out, out, damn Crisco . . ." I've never told anyone that story. I always though they'd think I was sick or something. But it was oddly beauti-ful; I know that in my heart—in spite of my shame.

Myron

I saw God in San Francisco once. I could introduce you—if I could find the place. It was pre-plague. Ten years ago. I went to this AA meeting—small, intimate, maybe twenty guys at the most. We sat in a circle and everyone told their story. I remember one guy talked about sleeping with his mother's bras and panties when she deserted him. Another guy talked about his drunk father fucking him in the ass when he was seven years old. Then there were your garden variety alkies who just drank to numb the pain—no particular pain, just plain pain. I can see the faces of those men; I can hear their voices. Some of them had beards with streaks of gray. Long, leftover hippie hair so clean you could smell it. One guy was bald, another bleached blond. There were the ones who sounded like truck drivers and the ones who sounded like movie goddesses. They were all trying to figure out what happened—what happened to us, why did we drink and drug ourselves into oblivion? Because it was the thing to do? Because we hated ourselves? Because we learned the behavior from our mommys and daddys? In that room, it didn't matter. Nothing mattered except our being together. It was the smallest, the tiniest, I ever felt in my life. And yet the most powerful. There was no competition, no resentment, no hatred, no fear. No color. At the end of this meeting, after people had thrown up their souls, we stood in a circle and held hands. I can feel the hands of the two men on either side of me. One of them had the rough, crusty hands of a construction worker, the other had the silken hands of someone who had only touched champagne glasses. This leather queen, as nellie as he was butch, led us in the Lord's Prayer. Maybe there was a candle in the room, casting shadows? I'm not sure but there was a presence—an aura?—hovering over this circle of queer men. It was shapeless but not colorless. Sometimes I remember it as golden, other times I remember red. It had to be God in that room. I began to cry, subtle tears, sneaking down my cheeks and along my neck, down my chest. I felt God. Or something. I felt something larger than I was, larger than anyone in the room, larger than mommy and daddy and all the pain in all of our lives. God was in San Francisco that night. I felt it, saw it, experienced it. Do you believe me?

MOVIE QUEEN

Charlie

Charlie is a gay man, 30 to 40, any ethnicity.

The last time I bumped into Joshua—and, honey, I do mean bumped into him—was at the Los Angeles County Museum. The movie theatre. What's it called? The Crosby? No, the Bing. There was a screening of Carolyn Jones in *Song of Bernadette.* I mean, Jennifer Jones. Carolyn was the one on the *Munsters.* Or was that Yvonne DeCarlo? Jennifer is the one married to Norton Simon. Another museum. Pasadena. Is Carolyn Jones still alive? Norton Simon died last year. I remember because it was the same day Joshua died. And I felt sorry for Jennifer Jones. Jennifer Jones was always surrounded by death. First, she was married to Robert Wagner. Who died of alcoholism. No, Robert Walker. Robert Wagner was married to Natalie Wood. Twice. Talk about surrounded by death. Did anyone ever figure that out? Joshua said she (Natalie) was drunk while Robert Walker was fucking Christopher Walken. I mean, Robert Wagner. Who's he fucking now? Jill St. John? Or is it Stephanie Powers? Who was the one who was with William Holden when he died? She wasn't with him, he was alone; but she was dating him, seeing him, whatever. Stella Stevens? Talk about a nasty death. Dead drunk. Smashed his head. Maybe that's how Robert Walker died, too. Then Jennifer Jones married Selznick, who produced—in addition to *Gone With the Wind*—*Song of Bernadette.* Which brings me back to Joshua. I should have known he was a Jennifer Jones fan. Anyway, he was not well that night he bumped into me. He wasn't drunk; he'd been in The Program for ten years (and wouldn't let any of us forget it). But he was very wobbly on his feet and painfully thin. I'd heard, of course, that he had It, but you're never prepared, are you? He and his friend sat near me and my friend. My friend and me. Before the movie started, Joshua started telling us these Jennifer Jones stories (he supposedly had a friend who'd worked at the Norton Simon Museum). Once, according to Joshua, she filled the bathtub with Oil of Olay and was shocked, after she emerged, hours later, feeling years younger, that the pink gunk wouldn't flow down the drain. Her maid had to empty the tub—shovel it out or something. Joshua swore he used Oil of Olay as a lubricant. To keep his pussy young, he said. Joshua was a little over-the-top that night, like he might have had a tad of dementia. But it would be hard to tell with him. I'll never forget when I first met him. We were standing in line in front of the Hollywood Wax Museum. I had been in town about fifteen minutes; he'd been in town about fifteen years. In all that time, he'd never been to the Hollywood Wax Museum. Anyway, we wound up not going; we went to his apartment behind Hamburger Hamlet instead. I could not believe the smell when he opened the door. The smell of old, musty newspapers. Which there were—everywhere—in addition to photographs of every star you've ever heard of, including some real obscure ones. There was not one square inch of wall uncovered: Judy, Marilyn, Michael Landon, Karen Carpenter, Hepburn (both of them), Donny Osmond, on and on and on. Probably Jennifer Jones, but I don't remember. And, smack in the middle of the room was a Plexiglas coffin of sorts. Well, not a coffin, a case. A Plexiglas case. With one of Julie Andrews' dresses from *The Sound of Music*. Honey, it was sick. I mean, who needed the Hollywood Wax Museum? Joshua was a trip and a half. That was pre-AIDS, pre-HIV, pre-weekly memorials. That was the first time I saw him; the last time was at *Song of Bernadette*. It's an incredible movie. About Lordes. About believing. About healing. Really spiritual. All during the movie, I couldn't imagine what Joshua was thinking. I was trying to remember if Shirley Jones really won an Oscar and for what movie. Was it Best Supporting Actress? Jennifer Jones did win—Best Actress—for *Song of Bernadette*. And in the final moments, that ethereal moment when she's released from her earthly pain, Joshua began sobbing. Not crying, like you do at the end of a movie; sniff-sniff-wipe-your-nose-with-your-popcorn-napkin. Really sobbing. Great buckets of tears. Popcorn buckets of tears. It must have been this amazing catharsis for him. He was a movie queen. He loved Hollywood. More than anyone I know. When he was a little boy, he dreamed of coming to Hollywood. And his dream came true. Like so many of us, he made his dream come true. Whenever I had a question about anything related to Hollywood, I'd call Joshua. He was Mr. Hollywood. Now he's gone. Released, like Bernadette. On the same day as Paul Simon. Norton Simon.

ROBERT'S MEMORIAL

Mel

Mel is an outrageous queen, thirty something.

Allow me to introduce myself: I'm Mel, Bob's best friend. And with Bob's help—she was a control queen if there ever was one—I've arranged today's memorial. He refused to call it a "celebration." "A celebration is when you drop a Quaalude and go to the Meat Rack," he was fond of saying. He also insisted there be no flowers. If he couldn't do the flowers, no one could. I thought of substituting fruit, infinitely more appropriate. We're going to begin with a little slide show I put together. Lights, please. Music, maestro. What's the matter? Technical difficulties so early in the show?—I mean, memorial. The bulb blew? What are the chances of that? Okay, Bobby, you win. He hated the slide show idea; he thought it was too Norma Desmond for words. So I guess he won. The light bulb blew? Are you sure? Did you try another plug? Turn off that music. I'm the only fag in the world who loathes Miss Sondheim. Bob loved him. He did not get through all of last year and he is not still here, thankyouverymuch. Well, that's show biz. I'm going to begin; we've asked that the speakers keep their comments brief so some of you can make it to the Beer Bust at The Gauntlet. I'll never forget when he pranced into our Positive Support meeting—get it? Positive Support? Brimming with double meaning—about three years ago. He said testing positive was like that moment in *The Wizard of Oz* when it goes from black and white into color. Hello? Who is this demented cookie? I thought to myself. When I tested positive for HIV, it reminded me of another one of Judy's hits: *Judgment at Nuremberg.* Anyway, it was only the first of many color references. If anything, Bob was color-ful. Full of color. Full of shit sometimes, too, as most of you know. I always told him the reason he became a florist is because it was the one occupation where he could look halfway butch. And it's true—dressed in those tight jeans and plaid shirts (she never recovered from the Village Idiot period; I mean, Village People) she looked like Clint Eastwood compared to some flower girls. But underneath that quasi-butch exterior lurked one loony leading lady. Last year, I got him a license plate for his birthday. F-F-A-W-W. Far From A Well Woman. I was also the one who talked him into doing drag. "You simply must before you die, honey," I pleaded. I mean, he'd been to Egypt, but he'd never walked down Santa Monica Boulevard in a dress; priorities, priorities. It was last Halloween. As it turned out, his last Halloween. I'll admit, at this point in his AIDS career, he was a little wobbly on his feet—even when he wasn't wearing three-inch stiletto pumps. Well, we were at the corner of Santa Monica and Crescent Heights in full regalia (he looked like an anorexic Loni Anderson), poised to cross the street when a car hit a skunk in the road (a real one, girlfriend—not one of the other drag queens) and the goddam thing sprayed all over us. Believe me, no amount of Liz's Passion would kill the smell. So we went to our respective homes, after stopping at the Seven-Eleven for several cans of tomato juice. You should have seen the clerk's face. We smelled like we'd been staying at the Coral Sands for a week. He probably thought we were going to have a few hundred Bloody Marys; we'd get so drunk we wouldn't have to smell each other. Tomato juice, they say, is the only way to get rid of skunk stench. Bob went to his house; I went to mine. We both plunged into a tub of tomato juice. Next thing I know, Bob's roommate—a drama queen with a capital "Q"—calls me on the phone, hysterical. "Bob's killed himself," she's screaming, very Olivia de Havilland. Well, I knew he was disappointed we weren't going to win the Costume Competition at Rage, but suicide? "I've already called 911," Olivia shrieks into the phone. Now I'm concerned. "I came home and found him in the bathtub, unconscious, lying in his own blood. He must have slashed his wrists." "Oh, Mary, get a grip," I said. "She got squirted by a skunk in West Hollywood." "Who? What's his name?" Olivia demanded. By this time, I hear sirens in the background; the paramedics have arrived to bandage Bob's wrists (not a bad idea all things considered). "Gotta go," Olivia chirped, as if it was a blind date she'd been expecting. Bob had fallen asleep in the bathtub. *Quelle surprise* to wake up to a pack of pumped-up paramedics staring down at her. She must have thought she'd died and arrived at heaven's bathhouse. Or Circus Books. When she emerged from the tub—like Marilyn in those clips from *Something's Got To Give*—revealing a constellation of k.s. lesions on her chest (very Tom Hanks), the paramedics split faster than you can say "Nazi." After it was all over, Olivia de Havilland had only one question: "Who was the skunk?" When Bob would tell the story, he'd describe it in Technicolor. The tomato juice wasn't red; it was "crimson." Bob, in fact, was crimson. Everything about him was red: bold, daring, alive, vibrant, sexy, passionate. The color of valentines; the color of roses; the color of Lucy's hair; the color of shoes; the color of blood; the color of tomato juice. When I got The Call—from Andy, his nurse—I thought back to that Halloween night. Another mistake, right? He can't be dead. But this time he really was. His heart—his crimson heart— had given out. Maybe I should have had "crimson" put on his license plate. *(Counting)* C-R-I-M-S-O-N. Seven letters. It would fit.

Claire

Claire is an ordinary, middle-aged woman from Dayton, Ohio.

I met Robert a couple of years ago; we were on a tour group
together, cruising down the Nile for nine days. Robert loved
to cruise. Is that funny? You guys have such a good sense of
humor. (I didn't understand half of what that Mel just said).
There were thirteen of us on the cruise: six couples and
Robert. My husband, Carl (who died two weeks ago—that's
another story), was pretty ill at the time and wasn't up to all
the daily activities: visiting mosques, exploring temples,
crawling through tombs. Since Robert was the odd man out
and I was the odd gal out, we'd wind up together; sitting
together on a bumpy bus ride to Aswan, eating lunch together at the hotel where *Death on the Nile* was filmed, standing
in a queue at the Cairo Museum. I wasn't complaining,
believe me. Robert was the most polite, the most handsome,
the most articulate, the most lively man in the group. I know
what you mean about the words he'd use to describe colors.
The colors or the hieroglyphics in the tombs became even
more magnificent when Robert described them. Yellow was
marigold; blue was periwinkle; green was emerald. Everyone
was constantly taking pictures—Robert would take pictures
of me; I'd take pictures of him. One day, he gave me a hint
which I was too dense to pick up on. "Claire," he said, "You
must take a picture of me under this sign." It was the
entrance to the Valley of the Queens. He then said he was
hoping to find the Valley of the Dolls. I didn't get it; I just
never picked up on the fact he was gay. I'd ignore comments
from some of the men who made fun of him—his being a
florist, the way he'd describe those colors, for instance. One

morning, before dawn, I was having trouble sleeping so I roamed up to the deck. There was Robert. At times it seemed like we were destined to be together—in the same place at the same time. That's when he told me he was gay. I have a gay nephew—one that I know of, anyway—so I'm not completely naïve. Gay-schmay; he was my new friend. As the sun crept up over the Nile, we watched the little villages come to life. Robert asked me what I thought about afterlife. We talked about the Egyptian culture and their heightened spirituality. As the light replaced the dark, we got into religion and reincarnation. I could talk to him about anything. "I'm going to tell the group," he announced. "I need to tell them I'm gay." It was like he wanted my permission. Which I gave him, of course. When he told his parents, they rejected him—especially his mother. Ever since then, he said, he couldn't keep it a secret. "I like to know where I stand," were the exact words he used. People in the group reacted politely—some were supportive, others were sorry he said it out loud. But everyone respected him—even this blowhard homophobe from Atlanta. I was happier than ever he was my unexpected date for the trip. Now I was exotic by association. After we got back to Ohio, Carl got worse. Cancer. A relapse. But he had fulfilled a dream by visiting Egypt before he died. So had Robert, I guess. But he hadn't told me that; he hadn't told he had death in his veins, just like my husband. It wasn't until about six months ago that he wrote me about the HIV which had begun to attack his body. We had engaged in a spirited correspondence, sending each other letters, cards, photographs, articles from the paper, comics, recipes; you-name-it, we shared it. He once asked me to mail him some fall leaves. You should have heard him rave about the colors: copper, scarlet, pumpkin. When I got that letter, I went to the library and read everything I could get my hands on about HIV and AIDS. Carl, meanwhile, was getting chemotherapy—again—and barely hanging on. There is a photograph of me with Robert, taken the last night on the ship. A costume party. He insisted on doing my hair and makeup for the occasion: several different colors of eye shadow, just the right color fingernails. He made me feel beautiful; I don't know what I looked like but I felt beautiful, like Cleopatra floating down the Nile. He's wearing a golden galibaya in the photo, one of his more outrageous purchases. "Where will you wear that in L.A.?" I asked him. "Grocery shopping," he said. We were both so happy. When I'd look at the photograph, I didn't fear death. Carl's death. Robert's death. My own death. That photo made me believe those Egyptians are right; there is something on the other side. Carl died two weeks ago. I'd begun talking to Robert on the phone once a week so I knew they were simultaneously on a downward spiral. Staring at the picture became my only solace. When Carl died, I knew it was time to say goodbye to Robert. On the same day that I buried my husband of twenty-eight years, I got on the phone and called Robert. Andy, his nurse, answered. At first, he thought I was Robert's mother. I was sorry to disappoint him. "Robert keeps thinking she'll call," he said. "If you're coming, you better hurry." I booked a flight to L.A. Even if there is an afterlife I wanted to see Robert one more time in this life. On the day I arrived, the day that Robert died, there was an earthquake. Here I am, this dame from Dayton, my first time in California, and the plane is circling over the airport because of an earthquake. Five something on the Richter scale. I could see smoke from fires, red lights from ambulances—signals of death. I kept thinking, "Don't let him die before I see him." We circled for hours. By the time I got to his house—shuttle, bus, cab—he was slipping. He was refusing to see anyone. Or maybe it was Andy who was refusing to let anyone see him. Everyone had said their goodbyes, Andy said—even Robert's father—but he still wouldn't die. "There's no earthly reason he should be alive," Andy kept saying. Andy hadn't told him I was coming. Andy wanted it to be a surprise. He was surprised; at first he didn't recognize me. Then he whispered,

"Hello, Cleopatra." He commented on my pantsuit: "Jungle red, Sylvia," he said. He looked beautiful—like a religious painting. I told him I was beginning to believe, more and more, in afterlife. He said he believed in destiny; he said that our friendship was fate. And then he just stopped. He didn't die; a part of him—the physical part—just stopped. We were holding hands. And he looked as happy as he did in that photo while we were floating down the Nile. And even though he didn't have on his golden galibaya, there was an aura, a golden presence filling the room, all glowing and tingling.

Brian

Brian, paunchy and pushing fifty, still maintains a certain star quality.

I was only with Robert on a precious few occasions: twenty years ago, about ten years ago, and a few weeks ago. He was only sixteen when I first met him. I was performing in St. Louis. The Ice Capades. I was one of the male leads—not only was it twenty years ago, it was at least twenty pounds ago. He had sent me a single lavender orchid in a brandy snifter which arrived backstage before a performance. "I'll be seeing the show tonight for the fifth time. You are the best. Bobby" was scrawled on the card. It was unusual to receive a card from a "Bobby"—most gifts were from enraptured young girls. So I wasn't completed surprised when, an hour after I returned to my room at the Forest Park Hotel, my phone rang and this kid says, "Hi, I'm Bobby. I'm in the lobby." Of course I was curious; a few seconds later, he appeared at the door: a gawky, skinny teenager with bad skin and bad hair. I couldn't believe how young he was. But believe me, he knew what he wanted. Me. I think it was because of my skating career; he was obsessed with the idea of being with an ice skater. He was a virgin; I was chosen to break the ice, as it were. I had never been in this situation before and I was not comfortable. He was determined, however, and eventually we were lying in bed with our clothes off. I took the orchid, which I'd brought home because it was just so perfect, and lightly touched every inch of his soft, white body with the delicate, feathery flower, hoping that would be enough for his first time. No way. "You make me feel beautiful," he said. He insisted we go further and I must say there was something so sure about him that made it okay—even though I had broken out in a cold sweat. "I know I'm gay," he kept saying, "I want you inside me." I was very gentle; it was like we were fastened together, glued together. He snuggled in my arms all night long. I asked about his parents. "I left a note," he said. As it turned out, the note was his coming out chapter and I was his co-star. We made love a couple more times during the week I was in St. Louis. He was a very quick learner. He told his mother he was in love with me—an announcement from which she obviously never recovered. I told him he would be "in love" lots of times. For several years, I'd get letters from him, confirming my prediction. And occasionally there'd be a photograph signalling his transformation from a boy to man, from Bobby to Robert. We eventually lost touch. I retired from skating and settled in San Francisco where I opened a magazine/stationery store in the Castro. I was pretty jaded in terms of seeing hot men striding in and out of my store. But I must say I looked twice—no, three times—when this confident hunk, who looked vaguely familiar, sauntered in. Great skin, great hair, the works. Much to my surprise, he looked too. "Brian?" he said, in that unmistakable lilting voice. The tables had definitely turned. Now he was the star and I was the hungry one. To tell the truth, I hadn't had much sex. Ever. On the road, the other guys would call me the "Ice Queen." These are the same "friends" who called me "Piggy Fleming" when I started gaining a few pounds. I never felt particularly horny but Robert's resurfacing—he was definitely "Robert" now, all cool charm—brought up some long lost longing. I closed the shop. We went to my apartment. I was very nervous; now I was the awkward virgin. And in some respects, I was. Even though I was forty something, there were certain things I had never done. I suppose I was a bit of an ice queen. Well, now I wanted him—Robert, the man—inside me. We had switched roles; he was no longer Lolita and I'd become Mrs. Robinson. The ice queen melted in his arms, under the weight of his newly acquired body. He made me feel hot, almost beautiful.

The next day a brandy snifter arrived at my shop, holding a perfect lavender orchid. No note, no words necessary. The next time I heard from Robert was about five years ago, delivering the news on my answering machine, his voice void of its usual cheer: "I tested positive. I thought you should know." A few weeks later, I left him the identical message: "I tested positive. I though you should know." Based on my sexual practices before and after that euphoric afternoon, there's little question I got it from Robert and that's simply what was meant to be. I do not regret. That's why I was so heartened to get the call, saying that he wanted to see me before he died. We were bound to each other—unmistakably, unremittingly joined—by some of life's most durable threads. Seeing him this time, the third time, he had reverted to Bobby, the skinny, unsophisticated teenager with unruly hair and unmanageable skin. When I arrived in L.A., he hadn't gone home yet; he was still in the hospital and was having a pretty rough time. I brought him an orchid, but he seemed too out of it to notice. I spent most of the night, soothing every inch of his fevered body with chunks of ice. "The ice queen cometh," he managed to say, in between involuntary naps. We didn't talk much; words to describe how I felt have yet to be invented. I just wanted to be with him, somehow linked to him. I've spent my entire life disengaged, disassociated, disconnected; I was present for every minute spent with Robert. Painfully, joyously alive. On all three occasions. At this final meeting, there were no explanations, no recriminations, no goodbyes, no weepy I-love-yous; after his fever broke that night, I snuggled in the hospital bed with him and left before dawn, while he was still asleep. On the evening he died, I got a cold chill. The phone call from Andy, a couple of hours later, only confirmed what my shivering body had informed me. I've yet to feel warm again; it's like there's ice water in my veins. Part of Bobby kept my insides warm. If I experienced passion, it was because of him, because of his heat, his fire. Extinguished.

Beverly

Beverly is an over-the-top actress, fortyish.

"Why do I always wear black? Because I am in mourning for my life." Masha in *The Three Sisters,* a role I was playing when I met Bobby baby. Today I wear black because I am in mourning for Bobby's life. I can hear him saying, "Make sure the blacks match. Not too much eye makeup. Not too much jewelry." I walked into his shop, about twelve years ago, and ordered myself an elaborate bouquet to be sent to the theatre where I was doing *Three Sisters.* He didn't blink; he didn't ask why I was ordering myself flowers; I guess he'd heard everything. But I decided to tell him. Those other two broads—the ones who played Irina and Olga—had boyfriends who would send them flowers. Bobby baby understood. "What name do you want on the card?" he asked. Well, I hadn't thought of a name. Leave it to Bobby baby to come up with the perfect one: Lenny. "Playful but important—possibly an agent," he said. "Or a married man. It's sexy." This was our first, but not our last, scheme together. He sent the flowers—spectacular. My two sisters were as green as the ferns. But here's the best: the following night, another huge bouquet arrived, with a car signed, "I saw your show last night and I need to fuck you. Bobby." It was a joke, of course; he wanted to do my hair more than he wanted to fuck me; we became immediate friends. Girlfriends. That's when I started calling him up "Bobbybaby": "Bobby, Bobby baby. Bobby booby. Bobby, come on over for dinner . . ." *Company*—one of the few Sondheims I haven't done. After he got to know me, Bobby said I'd been in training to play the Elaine Strich role since I was in kindergarten. Maybe one day I will and I'll dedicate the performance to him. I did *Merrily We Roll Along*, *Follies* (won a *Drama-Logue* award for that), and of course, Rose in *Gypsy*. B.B. Before Bette. Of course I'm far too young for the role, but not in Equity-waiver. Thank God he stayed alive to see it: "Some people got it and make it pay, some people can't even give it away, but this person's got it and this person's spreadin' it around . . ." He sent me dozens of long-stemmed roses. He was not well the night he came to the show. He was vomiting before, after, and during intermission. "In my case, everything's not comin' up roses," he said. He always brought me flowers to coincide with the role I was playing: daisies when I played Daisy in *Clear Day* ("Hey, buds below, up is where to grow, up with which below can't compare with . . .") When I did *Cactus Flower* (Goldie won an Oscar; I won my first *Drama-Logue* award), he sent a six-foot-tall cactus. He made me feel special; there is not a straight man in the world who could make me feel like he did. I am not a fag hag. Bobbybaby said that as long as I weighed less than two-hundred pounds and got laid at least twice a year, I was not a fag hag. Believe me, it's not been easy—avoiding fag hagdom, that is. Bobbybaby was always helping me with man trouble, something he could write a book about. I once had a blind date and insisted Bobbybaby show up at the restaurant—just in case the guy turned out to be a mass murderer. Well, I'm sitting there—with this very handsome man—and Bobby approaches the table, like a star-struck fan. "Miss Sparks," he says. "Can I have your auto-graph?" Meanwhile, he's checking out this guy—who is looking very uncomfortable. I nonchalantly sign the auto-graph, like it's something I do on a daily basis. A few minutes later, I'm being paged. I get to the phone and it's Bobby: "Bad news, honey, I fucked that queen at the baths less than a month ago." Well, that did it—I needed another closet case like I needed another calorie. No thanks. I just left the guy sitting there and met Bobby at a bar around the corner. It was very Lucy and Ethel. He took care of me. "I'm your Joseph von Sternberg, Marlene," he'd say. And he was. Sometimes it made me guilty because he seemed so much more comfortable taking care of me than he did taking care of himself. I didn't dare mention the "c" word: codependent. He hated twelve-step anything; he wanted to start a twelve-step meeting for people who refused to recover: "God, grant me the hysteria to reject the things I cannot change . . ." was his motto. And he'd refuse to listen to me talk about O.A. "You always have to weigh more than I do," he'd say. "It's in your contract." When Bobbybaby started to get sick, he refused to slow down. He kept working in addition to being my best friend (a full-time job in itself). But eventually there were days when he needed something from me. I'll never forget the first lesion on his nose. After all those years of him advising me on what shades of makeup to wear, I was standing at the cosmetic counter picking out the right base to camouflage his lesion. More and more, I realized our roles were reversing. I began to do things for him that I never did for myself— laundry, cooking, cleaning his house. I was offered the role of Vera in a waiver production of *Mame* opposite Adrienne Barbeau, but I turned it down. It was not an easy decision but he needed me. It was the first time in my life anyone needed me—other than audiences, of course. On the day of last year's *Drama-Logue* Awards, he went in the hospital. He was not breathing well at all. It was the first time in eleven years that we didn't go to the awards together. There was no way I could go by myself; I was at his side. Don't ask me how he did it, but when I got home from the hospital that night, there was this humongous bouquet with a card: "Sorry we missed the awards." It was signed, "Norman Maine." As the weeks went by, he spoke less and less. When he was moved home, wearing a wrist corsage he'd created from an orchid, I became part of the team who took care of him, along with the home-care nurses. There were times when I felt like I was watching myself in a movie. Was it really me spoon-feeding him his cereal? Was it really me pushing the wheelchair? Was it really me changing his diapers? I couldn't believe it. Even though he was dying, he was still giving, giving, giving. Giving me the opportunity to be unselfish, for the first time in my life. What a tricky bastard. I'll shut up now, promise—after I sing one of his favorite songs.

Andy

Andy is an African American male nurse, 30 to 50.

My name is Andy Love. I was Bobby's home-care nurse during the last month of his life. He introduced me as "Andy Divine Love." I was lucky to get to know some of you but really blessed to be a part of Bobby's life—even if it was for such a short time. You can't measure time, though, because you get intimate real quick when you're cleanin' somebody's butt several times a day. It was very hard for Bobby to be taken care of; he was not used to playin' that particular role. He spent his life takin' care of people. According to his friends, he was not only a florist, he was a psychiatrist. He was always involved in high drama—romances, births, weddings, funerals—and he did much more than arrange the flowers. In that way, we were very much alike. In fact, in spite of the obvious differences, were very much alike in many ways. "Sisters under the skin," he'd say. It's from a poem or something: "Rosie O'Grady and the Captain's Lady are sisters under the skin." Not only did I become very well acquainted with his physical pain during those final weeks, Bobby also let me in on his emotional shit. In the middle of the night, when he couldn't sleep, he'd tell me the stuff about his mother. I knew all about bein' rejected. My mama kicked me outta the house when she caught me havin' sex with one of her live-in boyfriends. The boyfriend stayed but she threw me out, she said, because I was a faggot. I'm not sure what that made him. I was fifteen and went to live with one of her brothers, my uncle, who put me up, took care of me and eventually put me through nursing school. He and his lover, that is. So Bobby and I shared this mother thing. One day he said,

"Even though I don't have anyone I can call 'mother,' I have a father who's cool and a lot of incredible friends." He was grateful for what he did have. Even though he was incontinent, burning up with fevers, unable to keep any food down, he'd suddenly announce, "I'm glad I'm not blind." Suddenly I realized he was playing the glad game. "You're a Hayley Mills fan!" I screamed. He was, of course. Well, that cemented our sisters-under-the-skin relationship. The glad game, for those of you who don't know, is from *Pollyanna.* No matter how dire the situation was, Hayley, as Pollyanna, would find something to be glad about. I've played the glad game all my life. Bobby, too. When I was a kid, I had pictures of Hayley Mills from fan magazines, Scotch-taped all over the walls of my bedroom. Bobby, too. Well, even though it was 4:00 A.M. when we were having this conversation, he sent me to the video store to pick up Hayley's best films—in addition to *Pollyanna,* I got *The Parent Trap,* and *The Trouble With Angels.* A Hayley Mills Film Festival of our very own. After watching these three films in a row, we realized why we were Hayley Mills fanatics. She starts out as a sweet, adorable little girl in *Pollyanna;* she falls in love with her mirror image as a result of severe family dysfunction in *The Parent Trap;* and in *The Trouble With Angels,* she winds up being a radical bitch. This was the story of our lives. Not only were Bobby and I sisters under the skin, we were identical twins. In *The Parent Trap,* there's a duet which Hayley sings to herself, playing both twins, called "Let's Get Together." Well, Bobby had me replay it about forty-five times, until we memorized every word and could sing along. "Let's get together, yeah, yeah, yeah. Why don't you and I combi-ine? Let's get together, whaddaya say? We could have a real good ti-ime. We'd be a cra-a-azy team. Why don't we ma-a-ake the scene—together?" It was one of the best nights of my life. When it became clear he only had a limited amount of time, he got very serious about who should get what and what should go where and what should be thrown away. It seems there was one task that only I could do. Several weeks prior, he'd filled a plastic bag with dildos which he wanted to get rid of. Problem was, there were some real whoppers and no matter how you stuffed them in the bag, anyone could see it was a bunch of gigantic rubber pricks. Even though he didn't have the strength to accomplish the task, he'd figured out what to do: chop them up with the pruning shears, so there would be no obvious protrusions sticking out from the plastic bag for the trash collectors to see. This gave new meaning to trash collectors, by the way. So there I was—where's Lorena Bobbitt when you need her?—slicing up dildos into small pieces. I went to nursing school for this? I was laughing so hard, I began crying. Crying—not only for the obvious reasons, but also because this meant he was going to die. I was honored to be the chopper of his dildos, but the thought of losing him was unbearable. We're not supposed to get too emotionally involved, blah, blah, blah. Tell me how you could not get emotionally involved with Bobby. When he died, about a week later, I took it pretty hard. My twin sister was gone. I tried to play the glad game—that's what Pollyanna would do. Even though the time with him was too short, I was glad Bobby happened to me; even though I felt more alone than I ever have in my life, I was glad to have been part of a cra-a-azy team; and even though he's not physically here anymore, I'm glad he will never let me forget him.

Robert Sr.

Robert Sr. is distinguished and handsome, still sexy at sixty something.

He was only eight or nine years old when he started bringing flowers home from the local cemetery. That's when we knew he was special. Different. Not like other boys his age. Sensitive. And creative. So creative. And defiant. Even after several heated reprimands, he'd continue to steal those flowers off graves of the dearly departed. "Dead people don't care about flowers," he'd insist. And he was right, of course. He never changed his mind—even after making a good part of his living by designing funeral arrangements. "They're for the living," he'd say. "That's why I charge them so much. It makes them feel good." Maybe that's why I don't feel so good today. I couldn't spend my money on flowers for my boy. My boy. The words seem so foreign, almost like another language. He was a boy—'til the day he died. And he was mine, my flesh and blood. A father doesn't expect to lose his son—even though I'd almost lost him once before. A father is supposed to save his son. Not me. I could not save my boy. When I heard Bobby was dying of AIDS, I felt impotent all over again—just like I had when we almost lost him twenty-five years ago. His mother and I took him to go ice skating in Forest Park one Sunday afternoon in the dead of winter. The park, blanketed in snow, was beautiful—it looked like a Christmas card—and it was so cold that the lakes had frozen over. This wasn't professional ice skating; it was pretend ice skating. Which means he wore shoes, not skates. He was never particularly athletic but he loved to prance around on the ice. And he was a daredevil. Always.

His mother and I watched him from our car which was parked a good distance from the lake. Every couple of minutes, he'd turn and wave. The he'd do something dramatic: a turn, a twist. As he got further away, it looked like he was approaching a section of the lake that hadn't completely frozen. Or was it a mirage? He turned and waved. Then he was gone. Gone. Disappeared. He'd plunged through the ice. My wife and I jumped from the car and began running toward him, alongside the lake. A crowd was beginning to form. He's dead, I thought to myself. My boy is dead. I could see a man moving toward the shattered section of ice, risking his life. I could see Bobby's head bobbing up and down, his skinny arms reaching up. There was no sound; it was like a silent movie. Dead still. By the time we reached him, the young man—blond with an athletic build—had pulled Bobby out of the water. He was carrying him toward us—sensing, I guess, we were his parents. Suddenly there was sound. Bobby was gasping; my wife was crying; the spectators were cheering the young blond man with a big, bushy moustache. I took off my big, heavy overcoat and wrapped Bobby in it. I had never, before or since, seen anyone shaking like he was. And he was blue (he'd have a name for the particular shade of blue). "How can we thank you?" my wife asked. I don't know why but she insisted on getting his name and address. His name was David. David Fraser. And he lived not far from the park. He had saved my son's life. He was a hero. I was not. When I held Bobby in my arms that day, carrying him back to the car, I realized how seldom I'd ever touched him. In ten years, I'd barely ever hugged him or had any physical contact with my son. I remember feeling very weak that day—not at all like a father, not deserving of a son. I felt like a failure. I could not get the face of Bobby's savior out of my head: his yellow hair and moustache, as yellow as corn; his ruddy complexion. The following week, without telling my wife, I went to see him. He invited me in. We had a few beers. One thing led to another. He was very attractive. He was everything I wasn't. I wanted to be him. We made love on the floor of his living room. He held me in his muscular arms, the arms which had saved my son, and I willingly submitted to him. He fucked me. I had never had sex with a man; I guess I'd thought of it, but this was the first time. A virgin. After it was over, I felt even worse. I felt weak, unmanly, impotent. I did not understand my feelings—how I could be so ecstatic during the sex and so guilty after it was over. I never told my wife, needless to say, but when Bob told us he was gay, I wondered if I had passed it on to him. My wife nearly had a nervous breakdown; did she hate homosexuality—fear it?—because she knew about me? She has refused to speak to him or have any contact with him ever since. I had never stopped having secretive sex with men since my magical afternoon with David Fraser. In the most unlikely places, I searched for him in every man I encountered: the color of his thick hair, the smoothness of his freckled skin, the timbre of his soothing voice. Surely my wife wondered where I was; there must have been hundreds of inexplicable late nights, never questioned; she didn't want to know. When Bob came out, I curtailed my fervent hunt in fear of being found out by my own son. It wasn't until Bob told me he was HIV-positive that I felt obligated to reveal myself. Where did he get such courage with such a coward for a father? I knew who he was, yet it took the threat of losing him for me to let him know who I was. You know Bobby—he wasn't particularly surprised, but he was very . . . what's the word? . . . fatherly. He lectured me, not only about safe sex but about the importance of coming out. Silence equals death and all that. I finally divorced my wife and, as Bobby's life as a gay man was ending, my life as a gay man—an openly gay man—began. Bobby rescued me. Saved my life. But I couldn't save his. When I watched Bob dying, I felt those helpless feelings again. I wanted to be the one who could keep him alive, grab him from death's grip, wrap him in my overcoat and grasp him in my arms. But studying his face, there wasn't a trace of the panicked, shivering little boy of years ago. His face radiated a warm calm. Bobby did not need to be rescued; like life, he embraced death with an awesome acceptance. Which he tried to pass on to anyone lucky enough to brush up against him, including his father. Thank you for inviting me here today, thank you for allowing me to be a part of his true family.

DISCO DAZE

Danny

Danny is a gay white male in his forties.

It happened in 1976: The Accident. I was in my early twenties, still living with my parents who didn't know I was gay. I was on a date with this out-of-work actor named Luke. We went to the Backlot at Studio One to see Wayland Flowers and Madame. Opening night. Craig Russell, the female impersonator, was in the audience. And Peter Allen. And Rock Hudson! After the show, Luke and I went into the disco. We were dancing our asses off, sweating our brains out, under these incredible psychedelic lights. We weren't high—just a couple of glasses of white wine during the show. And a couple of snorts of amyl on the dance floor. We were ecstatic. The last thing I remember is hearing Sylvester singing, "You make me feel, so unreal . . ." Then blackness, nothing, a void. I didn't wake up until a week ago, almost twenty years later, with my parents (now in their sixties) standing over me. Patiently, they told me what happened: it seems one of those glittery disco balls unfastened from the ceiling and crash-landed on my head. That was all she wrote. I never regained consciousness. In fact, it was my mother who insisted I stay hooked up to machines; she believed I would recover. And, as it turned out, she was right. A miracle of sorts. The day after I came to, my parents threw this huge party; all our relatives and their friends came to get a look at me. Now I had no idea if my parents simply assumed I was gay since the accident happened at Studio One—one of the most notorious gay discos in the world. They settled out of court, by the way. I was anxious to see my Uncle Alex, one of my mother's brothers, who I knew to be as gay as a goose. An English teacher. Very funny and campy. But he didn't show up at the party; I was disappointed because I thought I'd at least have someone to confide in. There was a cousin I also suspected, Lisa, who did turn up at my coming-to party with her "roommate." I figured they were lovers which was confirmed in my mind by the fact they wore these cute little red ribbons. What a great code to let people know! Later in the night, this newscaster from the TV news showed up to do a story on me and he was wearing a red ribbon, too! I thought that was pretty bold. You wouldn't have seen that in 1976. After the party was over, I asked my mom about Uncle Alex. Her face just fell and she remained silent. "He didn't die, did he?" I asked. She began crying, then weeping, then sobbing. He must have been pretty young, I said. "About to turn forty," she said. For a brief minute, I thought maybe he got hit in the head by a disco ball, but I knew it couldn't happen twice to one family. "Car accident?" I asked. "I'll tell you about it later," she said. I slept great that night, even though it was unsettling to think that my favorite uncle had died at such an early age and here I was, for whatever reason, alive. I had a dream about my Uncle Alex: we were having sex in a field of flowers, white flowers, and it started raining, lightly at first and then pouring. We just kept making love as the flowers turned red. Then it seemed the flowers were bleeding. And we were both bleeding—my uncle and I. When I woke up, my stomach was all wet. I thought it was blood but it was cum—my cum, my uncle's cum. I knew it was time to explore the city. I couldn't believe my eyes at the breakfast table: my mom was wearing a red ribbon! This was amazing to me—my mom, a lesbian? And so open about it, wearing it in front of my dad? Times had definitely changed. I guess my dad's probably bi (wonder what color ribbon indicates that). Before venturing out, I called several of my old friends; their numbers were either disconnected or belonged to someone else. Or no one was home. That night, I made myself a red ribbon, put it on one of my old plaid shirts and headed for Studio One, like a criminal returning to the scene of the crime. Only I wasn't a criminal. The first thing that surprised me was that I was the only one at Studio One wearing a red ribbon—even though everyone looked pretty gay. The first guy I spoke to was really a character. I asked him why no one was wearing red ribbons. "The same reason they're not wearing plaid shirts, doll," he said, referring to my outfit. He was sarcastic but I kinda liked him. He was wearing a T-shirt that said, "Positively Angry." I didn't get it. Trying to explain my clothes, I told him that I'd been laid up for quite a while. "Pneumacystis?" he said, like he was guessing the winning answer on a game show. Before I could answer, he said, "Me, too." Then he said, "How long have you been positive?" I tried to explain: "After spending the past twenty years in bed, I have every reason to be positive." He looked somewhat taken aback. "You can say that again, honey." Then he asked me some more questions which I really didn't understand. Like, did I take AZT? I assumed it was like LSD so I said no, I didn't like to hallucinate; he said he understood. Then he asked if I was doing anything prophylactically. I thought he said "prophetically," so I asked if he meant like going to a psychic. "You're a trip," he said, an expression I remembered from the seventies. After a few more minutes of conversation, he said he thought it was really cool that someone with dementia had the guts to go out in public. He just hoped I wasn't driving. When I told him I thought it was safer for me to drive than to go on the dance floor, he screamed. Then he excused himself. The next fellow I met had a little black square thing attached to his belt. When I asked what it was, he looked at me like I was from Mars. "It's a beeper. I'm a masseur." "Gosh," I said, "I could use a massage. I've been flat on my back for almost twenty years." He laughed. "You and I have a lot in common," he said. I asked him how much he charged and he said it depended on what I wanted to do. Then, like the other guy, he asked me about being positive. I told him I was "very positive." "Well, I won't do anything unsafe." That's good, I thought to myself. Then he handed me a card with a real glamorous photo of him. It said, "All Scenes, Call Brad." When I said, "I thought you were a masseur, not an actor," he gave me this bewildered look and split. Actually I was hoping to run into Luke, the actor I was dating when the accident happened. To tell the truth, I didn't see one single person I knew from the seventies. Not one. I must admit I was getting all overwrought looking at all these guys, so I approached this man who looked more accessible than most. I asked him if, by any chance, he knew of an actor named Luke. I described him: blonde, blue-eyed, extremely beautiful, tall. "Of course, I know him," he said. "His death changed history—even though he was a major closet case." Death? He died? Luke is dead? "He was the most famous actor to come down with it; everyone was forced to pay attention." "Come down with what?" I asked. Then I tried to explain that I'd been in a coma for twenty years. "You're fuckin' lucky," he said, as he made an excuse to move on. The idea that Luke was dead on top of hearing that my Uncle Alex was dead just made me hornier than ever. When this guy approached me, I was really ready. "I'm negative," he said, after a few minutes of conversation. I just couldn't believe it—I mean, he was very pleasant, very enthusiastic—nothing negative about him. I told him how positive I was and he suggested it was probably better if I got together with someone else who was positive. He was really so sweet about it. And comforting. Almost guilty. I don't know where he got the idea he was negative. So, anyway, I set out to find someone positive. It was easy. Paul. He was kinda skinny and he had a rash of some sort on his face, but he was still very handsome. I decided to take this guy home since he didn't have a place. I told him that I had just found out my mom was a lesbian, so I knew it would be cool. He said there was only one thing he had to tell me: he didn't have any rubbers, but it probably didn't matter since we were both positive. I agreed, completely confused, but going along with him. "And I doubt my Dad has any rubbers since my

Mom is now a dyke." He asked me if I was "for real" and told me that he meant it as a compliment. Since I hadn't told him about my accident or the coma, he was a bit confused when he saw my room. "Truly retro, dude," he said, looking at a movie poster of Stallone in *Rocky*. The only music I had was the most recent tape I'd bought: the soundtrack from Streisand's *A Star Is Born*. "You really are into the seventies, aren't you?" he said. When he took his clothes off, even in the dim moonlight I could see that rash was all over his body. And he had this thing attached to his chest. I didn't know what it was. Maybe some kind of nineties jewelry? There was a lot of that at the bar. It didn't matter. Paul was the best. The sweetest, the gentlest. He proved that. We made love all night as Barbra sang, "Love, soft as an easy chair." Imagine: I hadn't been penetrated, *fucked,* by a man ever in my life; imagine how good it felt, over and over and over. Sometimes we'd have to stop and he'd cough. Really bad. He must have fucked me five or six times—I lost count by the time the sun came up. He told me it was "the steroids." But it was great. He was so passionate, so caring. Sometimes I'd imagine I was being fucked by Luke. Or making love to Uncle Alex. I just wanted nothing more than for him to keep coming inside me, making me feel so fucking alive.